Imagination Besieged

Imagination Besieged records the silenced stories of a Mediterranean defined by loss, displacement, dispossession, violence, and its refusal. Drawing links and connections between Calabria, Athens, Ramallah, and Beirut, the book grapples with the legacies of histories of violence, criminality, and colonialism that define not only the past, but very much the present of a Mediterranean stuck in cycles of crises and death. This atmosphere of impossibility and immobility, as the author argues, debilitates and distorts imagination as much as it forces those subjected to it to find ways to express their dissent, sometimes in tragic ways.

The book invites to read with the "Mediterranean" as a space where violence can be "felt" and "breathed" in the air. It looks and makes connections between the works of artists and writers who have problematised and challenged existing ahistorical representation of the "Mediterranean" as an exotic tourist destination. In the works and words of the artists and writers discussed, the Mediterranean appears not as a mythical place, but in all its ambiguousness, paradoxes, dissonances, and the distortions on the bodies, the landscape, the environment, and the imagination produced by this persistent and invisibilised systemic violence. At the same time, *Imagination Besieged* listen to the refusal of this violence in the lives and practices of those who have rejected familial belongings, narrow definitions of identity, and their continuous dispossession.

Each essay taps into the depth of the archive of the modern Mediterranean to bring into the present what this present seeks to conceal.

Federica Bueti is the author of *Critical Poetics of Feminist Refusals: Voicing Dissent Across Differences* (Routledge, 2022). She is a lecturer of anthropology at UniCal, Reggio Calabria, Italy, and a Writing Tutor at the MA of Fine Art at Piet Zwart Institute, Rotterdam, the Netherlands. She has wide-ranging interests in decolonial, feminist, and Mediterranean literature, with particular focus on the decolonial feminist poetics and aesthetics of refusal.

Routledge Focus on Literature

Tolkien and the Kalevala
Jyrki Korpua

Elevating Humanity via Africana Womanism
Clenora Hudson (Weems)

Reading Modernity, Modernism and Religion Today
Spinoza and Van Gogh
Patrick Grant

The Sagas of Icelanders
An Introduction to All Forty Sagas with Summaries
Annette Lassen

Pandemics and Apocalypse in World Literature
The Hope for Planetary Salvation
William Franke

Reading Kazuo Ishiguro's *Never Let Me Go*
The Alternative Dystopian Imagination
Eva Pelayo Sañudo

Romantic Responses to Revolution through Miltonic Ideas of the Fall
Callum Fraser

Imagination Besieged
Coloniality, Violence, and Feminism in "Mediterranean" Art and Literature
Federica Bueti

For more information about this series, please visit: www.routledge.com/Routledge-Focus-on-Literature/book-series/RFLT

Imagination Besieged
Coloniality, Violence, and Feminism in "Mediterranean" Art and Literature

Federica Bueti

NEW YORK AND LONDON

First published 2025
by Routledge
605 Third Avenue, New York, NY 10158

and by Routledge
4 Park Square, Milton Park, Abingdon, Oxon, OX14 4RN

Routledge is an imprint of the Taylor & Francis Group, an informa business

© 2025 Federica Bueti

The right of Federica Bueti to be identified as author of this work has been asserted in accordance with sections 77 and 78 of the Copyright, Designs and Patents Act 1988.

All rights reserved. No part of this book may be reprinted or reproduced or utilised in any form or by any electronic, mechanical, or other means, now known or hereafter invented, including photocopying and recording, or in any information storage or retrieval system, without permission in writing from the publishers.

Trademark notice: Product or corporate names may be trademarks or registered trademarks, and are used only for identification and explanation without intent to infringe.

Library of Congress Cataloging-in-Publication Data
Names: Bueti, Federica, 1982- author.
Title: Imagination besieged : coloniality, violence, and feminism in "Mediterranean" Art and literature / Federica Bueti.
Description: New York, NY : Routledge, 2025. | Series: Routledge focus on literature | Includes bibliographical references and index.
Identifiers: LCCN 2024057027 | ISBN 9781032795423 (hardback) | ISBN 9781032795447 (paperback) | ISBN 9781003492634 (ebook)
Subjects: LCSH: Mediterranean Region--Literatures--History and criticism. | Violence in literature. | Imperialism in literature. |
Art--Mediterranean Region. | Violence in art. | Imperialism in art. |
LCGFT: Literary criticism. | Art criticism.
Classification: LCC PN849.M42 B84 2025 | DDC 809/.891822--dc23/eng/20241231
LC record available at https://lccn.loc.gov/2024057027

ISBN: 9781032795423 (hbk)
ISBN: 9781032795447 (pbk)
ISBN: 9781003492634 (ebk)

DOI: 10.4324/9781003492634

Typeset in Times New Roman
by KnowledgeWorks Global Ltd.

This book is dedicated to the loving memories of Angela Bueti, Pietro Bellantone, and Heiko Thandeka Ncube. Their passing is an immense loss for their loved ones, friends, and communities.

I dedicate this book to my parents, who taught me to love and never forget, yet be critical of my roots; to my region, this troubled land; to my sister Domenica and my nephews Ludovico and Alessandro; and to Shuruq Harb for being by my side as a friend and co-conspirator. Her practice is an invaluable source of inspiration. To Abdulkareem Al-Qabbani, whose dreams of justice and freedom for the Syrian people have lit the long nights of writing with their fire. To Jan Verwoert for always being supportive and generous with feedback. To Ozlem Altin, Onur Cimen, Anastasia Diavasti, Daniel Hui, Eirini Fountedaki, Urok Shirhan, Felipe Steinberg, Katarina Zdjelar, for sharing thoughts, conversations, and unconditional love, and for the encouragement to keep writing. To Vito Teti, whose acumen in observing the realities of Calabria has profoundly influenced my way of looking and convinced me to write this book.

To the future generations of Calabrians, because they might continue the work of listening carefully to the untold stories and histories' unexpressed potentials. I dedicate this book to the Palestinians and their struggle for freedom and self-determination, every day a bit closer, from the river to the sea.

Contents

0	Like Stubborn Fires	1
1	*Sciarra* (After Angela) I	15
2	*Sciarra* (After Angela) II	27
3	Movement I: From Grief to Grievance	33
4	Movement II: Even When They Are Dangerous, Examine the Heart of Those Machines You Hate	42
5	Colourless Knickknacks (After Fanon)	51
6	Living with Ruins	62
7	The Death Deal	71
8	Imagination Besieged	80
9	Movements at Sea: (Annotations on "Off You Shore Paper Trail")	90
	Bibliography	*101*
	Index	*107*

0 Like Stubborn Fires[1]

Edouard Glissant once noted that a population "whose domination by an Other is concealed, must search elsewhere for the principle of domination … because the system of domination … is not directly tangible."[2] The intangibility of the system of oppression becomes the necessity to craft a language that can disclose what has been concealed and is not immediately present to the oppressed, yet preserve the opacity and subversive gesture of disclosure. A language that can render tangible the opacities that imperial formation produces but also break free from it by searching for a "home" outside the given notions of origins, belonging, and identity. And in this landscape defined by displacement and dislocation, poetic diversion is a way of looking out of one's own country for a literary "home" which relies upon blending, fusion, improvisation, and hybridity.

The essays collected in *Imagination Besieged* listen for and pay attention to the presence of violence perceived as an all-pervasive absence, as that which "imperial architects disavow as not of their making."[3] The essays listen to the echoes of stories that were not meant to be told; stories that take place in a geography of "elsewheres" where we're simultaneously at home and foreigners. Stories that revisit the past, notions of home and belonging, to better understand the constraints still in force in and defining the present.

The stories that are witnessed here emerge within and disclose a Mediterranean geography of violence and toxicities that profoundly shape the sense of reality and possibility of the protagonists. The essays construct a geography which links the past and the present, and the faiths of countries across the Mediterranean Sea—Calabria, Greece, Lebanon, and Palestine. The narrators of these stories follow the traces and ruins of the nation-state, the impact of the European unfinished project of modernisation.

Many of the works discussed and the stories narrated are set against the backdrop of the aftermath of crises: the catastrophic events that led Calabrians to abandon the mountains and move to the coasts or migrate; the crisis brought by the process of modernisation; civil wars and conflicts; settler colonialism; the occupation of Palestine; the economic and social collapse of Europe; the migration crisis; and rebellions and murders which have left

DOI: 10.4324/9781003492634-1

2 *Imagination Besieged*

deep scars in the different communities living across the shores of the Mediterranean Sea.

The departing point of this study is the disappearance of the author's grandaunt, Angela Bueti, in the late '70s, in the mountains of Calabria, in Aspromonte. Little is known about the events that led to her disappearance. But like other similar cases, as a woman and a Calabrian peasant, Angela was victim of intersecting forms of violence. This violence continues, as we will see, in the present, producing immense losses for the local communities. The loss which Angela's murder faces the author with, and the impossibility of retrieving the pieces of evidence, or any information linked to her disappearance, on the one hand, makes it impossible to retell the story from Angela's perspective; on the other hand, it has prompted the need to reckon with the realities and the histories of violence and loss her disappearance resonates with.

To think with loss is a possibility to problematise the history of a land and a society which has normalised violence. The story of my grandaunt becomes the possibility to interrogate and problematise the history of my region: of the formation of the Italian nation-state and its imagined cultural community, created post-fact through the myths of its Greek-Roman inheritance; it's the history of the "othering" of the entire population for the sake of the imperial nation; the normalisation of violence against women and marginalised subjectivities who, like Angela, had rebelled to their destiny within their community, or context of criminality. They had refused abuses and aggressions and have paid, sometimes with their lives, their refusal of colonial, sectarian, and patriarchal violence.

Angela has enabled the possibility to speak of the many promises and failures of progress; the invisible presence of the 'ndrangheta in everyday life. This criminal organisation, as anthropologist Vito Teti has argued, is not only active in controlling the economic fate of the region but also "interferes in emotions ... 'ndrangheta has the perverse ability, almost the dominion on affects, a sort of magical power."[4] The presence of 'ndrangheta in Calabria can be felt, just like Angela's disappearance, as an absence, or a magical, intoxicating atmosphere of aggression, intimidation, and violence that suffocates the aspirations of individuals and entire communities and stiffens the ability of society at large to operate and imagine an existence outside the framework of this logic of privilege, honour, and shame.

What else was the disappearance of my grandaunt but an act of intimidation to instil fear and secure total control? This story is re-narrated in Chapters 1 and 2, respectively, in a series of poems titled *Sciarra (After Angela) I* and in an essay, *Sciarra (After Angela) II*. The impossibility to overcome this sense of loss for Angela's disappearance becomes the author's meditation on the impossibility to move on, to accept the normalisation of violence against women, marginalised communities, and the dissolution of the social fabric. The essay focuses on the historical roots of this sense of "loss" and of anger

Like Stubborn Fires 3

as morbid symptoms of those histories of violence, their effects on emotions, affects, interpersonal relationships, and the environment.

At the same time, the author's act of retelling this story, opens a space to address the realities and histories of violence that have formed her "identity" as Calabrian. While reflecting with other authors on this act of witnessing violence as an act of refusal, I become *implicated* witness to the realities of my region. "Implicated-ness" is here the awareness of my "complicity" with those structures of power and privilege that I discuss. In this respect, my way of seeing is "'folded into' (im-pli-cated in) events that at first seem beyond our agency as individual subjects." [5] Coming from the Northern shore of the Mediterranean, while I've always been perceived as a "southerner" in relation to the geography of Europe, in fact, within the Mediterranean region, Calabria "belongs" to the Northern shore, with all colonial implications. It means that the way I learnt of/with/on/the Mediterranean has been shaped by the hegemonic discourse of Western culture, which identifies in the Greek-Roman ruins and cultural heritage the origins of Western civilisation.

This epistemic violence is at the roots of many divisions and the impossibility of a "common" way of seeing. In this respect, I acknowledge the hegemonic subject position I speak from, and the limitation of my way of seeing. At the same time, I recognise commonality in the ways in which the empire has developed and used differences as a form of domination, within and outside its European borders. Othering is part of the survival mechanisms of empire, and as such it is important to keep interrogating it.

At the same time, with the word "implicated" I here refer to my participation in and intimacy with the realities narrated. I am not an external observer.[6] I've engaged in participant observations of these realities. I discuss my personal experience of the dissonances that animate the realities of growing up in the central Mediterranean frontier of Europe, which helps build the ground for this study. I've drawn, in my observation of Calabria, on the insights offered by the critical works of Corrado Alvaro,[7] and the anthropological studies of Vito Teti,[8] whose works witnessed with critical acumen and empathy the material and historical realities that have shaped "Calabrian identity" and by extension a certain image of the "Mediterranean type."

And through their eyes and stories, like Alvaro's Melusina, who lives, with a sense of disorientation, fear, alienation, the transformation Southern Italy underwent with the process of modernisation, I've re-narrated those stories, listening to the grief and the grievances, the optimism and the despair, grappling with the contradictions, and the unexplored potentials of alternative modernities.

Imagination Besieged is an act of witnessing—within my own writing process and in conversation with other writers—the quotidian realities of violence, loss, anger, depression, and melancholia in the context of the legacies of empire in the Mediterranean. Moving between autobiography, poetry,

4   *Imagination Besieged*

ethnographic accounts, and sociological reflections, together the essays in the book construct a map of Mediterranean "toxicities," where the Mediterranean is reflected in the psycho-affective landscape of stasis and urgency that defines it as a space of a radical distance.

The story of my grandaunt, while firmly situating my position within the frontier region of the central Mediterranean, also becomes an "excuse," or a "diversion" to address the larger question of how the Mediterranean and the identities of the Mediterranean have been imagined, invented, and reinvented over the course of more than two centuries, since Napoleon's invasion of Egypt and its occupation of South of Italy, by intellectuals, anthropologists, historians, artists, and poets from both North and South.

In *Maledetto Sud*, Calabrian anthropologist Vito Teti observes that, in the golden age of the Grand Tour, the region was constructed and perceived as a place of extreme and radical distance and that the many foreign travellers, who ventured through the "extreme" provinces, were placed on guard against going to the "cursed lands": described by the Jesuits as the "Indias de por acà" (The Indias of Here), where the inhabitants appeared "all from the forest," as in 1561 Giovanni Xavier wrote; or Calabria "Africa," seen as an exotic and difficult place to reach. Calabrians were described by foreigners as "barbarian, primitive, degenerate, senile, degraded, cursed, filthy, idle, brigand, nostalgic, violent, excessive, ambiguous, criminal, superstitious," even before they were able to speak for themselves.

Born in the age of European Imperialism, scholar Claudio Fogu argues, the Italian nation constituted itself into an "Empire State" that constructed its own south as Africa.[9] He has shown how this construction of the pathological "other," melancholic and prone to violence, was central to the imperial discourse and project. The "Mediterranean" here is thus more than a geography. It is a contested space; an idea loaded with the histories of colonialism; the struggle and revolts for the land, border violence, and control. It is a question of ways of seeing and the kind of narratives that are produced; of whom is looking and who is looked at; who is speaking and who is listening.

In the *Wretched of the Earth*, Fanon, who is an important influence and reference for this study, criticises the idea of a "Mediterranean community"[10] as a "cure" to the diseases of fascism and colonialism. He observes that all the words poured by European intellectuals in imagining an ideal "Mediterranean community" sounded like "dead-words" and "colorless knickknacks" to the ears of Algerians, who only knew too well the colonising cultural mission of the French nation. The coloniser can only laugh, Fanon observes when the values of "humanity," "beauty," and "hospitality" are mentioned, and with this laughter, he strenuously opposes them, disclosing the epistemic violence behind such ideals.

Following on the path opened by Fanon's decolonial approach, each essay observes and problematises the colonial matrix of power behind the discourse on the Mediterranean and, at the same time, listens to the undertones of this violence in the lives of the protagonists, in the "magical" atmosphere in which they're forced to live; and in the instances of refusal that offer them fleeting moments of "freedom." I here adopt Tina Campt's definition of refusal. She writes, "a refusal to recognize a system that renders you fundamentally illegible and unintelligible; the decision to reject the terms of diminished subjecthood with which one is presented, using negation as a generative and creative source of disorderly power to embrace the possibility of living otherwise."[11] Indeed, the protagonists of the stories and the works discussed are confronted by the deadly logic of nationalism, foreign interventions, sectarianism,[12] and regional rivalries live in the aftermath of colonisation and the post-colonial condition of perennial crisis.

In the conditions of oppression artificially created and maintained by the colonisers, their refusal doesn't necessarily manifest in their joining the revolutionary struggle. Refusal here manifests, Fanon observes, as a twitch, a muscular tension, as feelings of depression, anger, and a melancholic disposition. In this respect, the protagonists of these stories refuse with their whole bodies and lives. They are the incarnation of aspirations and desires that are forbidden to them and that they manifest in small acts of rebellion. Their refusal shapes and frames the storytelling.

The book follows on the path of the Mediterranean observed through the decolonising eye of Fanon and of post-colonial critics who have exposed and problematised the limitations of the Western way of observing the Mediterranean. In retelling those stories, *Imagination Besieged* taps into the deep fluid archive that is the Mediterranean to listen to the voices of those whose stories have been silenced; stories that both problematise the Mediterranean's legacies of empire and imagine alternatives.

As Predrag Matvejevic observes, the Mediterranean must be imagined and narrated not as an exclusively Latin, Roman, or Romance creation, or "from a purely pan-Hellenic, pan-Arab, or Zionist point of view, that is, on the basis of a particularist criterion, be it ethnic, religious, or political." And continues, "Our image of the Mediterranean has been distorted by fanatic tribunals and biased exegetes, by scholars without convictions and preachers without faith, by official chroniclers and court poets. Churches and states, prelates and kings, legislators ecclesiastical and Solomon's temple."[13] The Mediterranean is thus for Matvejevic neither simply a geography nor only history nor sense of belonging only. It is, as he insists, an archive. And within this archive, as anthropologist Iain Chambers argues, there exists a possibility "to narrate a modernity that is neither simply multiple nor, as its tri-continental formation underlines, merely a European matter."[14]

Chambers insists that we work with the idea of the Mediterranean as a question, a way of problematising the given narratives and images that obfuscate their complexity, contradictions, and plurality. He argues that, along "the economic and social registration of migration, racism and ethnonationalism... the Mediterranean enacts a radical undoing of the existing

6 *Imagination Besieged*

chains of meaning." And, in questioning the Eurocentric idea of the Mediter-ranean, national narratives are exposed for what they try to exclude. "The West, as the measure of the world, is undone. [...] The European 'home', its archives and histories, now exposed to the winds that blow across its land-scapes and seascapes, begin to shake under the gusts of what it is ontologi-cally unable to register and respond to."[15]

To think with the Mediterranean as an immense archive is thus to grap-ple with the complex and disquieting histories of modernity itself and think with those stories that have been neglected, negated, and repressed. It is, as Chambers suggestively writes, "go[ing] off-shore and float in its diverse cur-rents; is to consider the manner in which it constitutes an interrogative archive and counter-space to the prevalent understanding of modern Europe."[16] This Mediterranean archive becomes a site where "we can consider how its mul-tiple histories and cultural formations propose a diverse series of maps and coordinates." A site of possible re-elaborations and re-narrations of fragments of history that can help construct an alternative sense of the present.

The book takes seriously Chambers' exhortation to interrogate the Medi-terranean as an archive of multiple histories, and Sayidia Hartman's invitation to pay attention to how, in the archive, "those inside the circle listened for love and disappointment, the longing and the outrage," and "that fueled this collective utterance by the silenced and the silence."[17] How do silenced and marginalised voices narrate and interrogate the deep archive of the Mediter-ranean; how have they translated rage, longing, love, disappointment, and the sense of impossibility? Where did they find a language to explore and express affects that are less than hope and subtler than despair?

Following Chambers and Hartman's invitations to continue interrogat-ing and suggesting alternative storytelling that does justice to the silenced, *Imagination Besieged* records the stories of Angela, Marie Rose, and Abu Eyad, among other micro-narratives of defeat and resistance; of individuals who have experienced loss, dispossession, displacement, sexual and racial violence, and have found ways to express their dissent, sometimes in tragic ways. In retelling these stories, each essay pays attention to those absences, gaps, and silences; tapping into the depth of the archive to bring into the pre-sent precisely what this present seeks to conceal.

These obfuscations demand a different way of listening to what is being seen in this Mediterranean archive. It requires entering this large speculative archive and listening carefully to the worlds the narrators imagine, to the deep resonances those stories make, and to how they hold space for the unknown and uncertain, refusing given narratives of belonging, "home," "identity," and as Glissant insists, think with hybridisation, creolisation, with the idea of be-coming "an adoptive son," problematising the idea of roots and filiation.

In Chapters 3 and 4, I discuss "loss" as emotional dispositions and "anger" as a response historically and politically rooted in the histories of displacement, dispossession, and the histories of racism. Fanon's critique,

Like Stubborn Fires 7

as scholar Nouri Gana's insightful book *Melancholy Acts* argues, sets out to deconstruct and demystify the allegedly congenital aggressivity of the natives and "to explain the unorthodox behaviour of the Algerian who is prey to melancholia."[18]In the colonial context, Fanon argues unequivocally everything, including psychic pathologies, ought to be mobilised for the purpose of decolonisation.[19] Similarly, in her "Uses of Anger" and within the context of African-American struggle against white supremacy, Audre Lorde and other black and radical feminists insisted on the politicisation of effects for the purpose of the struggle for liberation. Lorde insists on de-pathologising anger,[20] exhorting white feminists to listen to the anger of their black sisters as a source of insights and collective mobilisation in the context of the larger struggle for liberation.

For Lorde, the point is how to learn to orchestrate that fury so that they might become insightful and liberatory, as these "opacities" demand places in which we can listen together to the traces of racism in everyday life as experienced by black and brown bodies. In both Fanon and Lorde, anger, aggressiveness, and melancholy as "individual dispositions" are read as manifestations of structural violence and as responses to a violence that is ongoing, pervasive, and persistent.

The liberatory and political currency that both thinkers attributed to emotions are problematised here and discussed in relation to the traumatic legacies of histories of violence in Algeria, Lebanon, Palestine, and Southern Italy. If imagination is, as feminists such as Cixous and Lorde have argued, the location for a possible liberatory politics, the essays ask what happens when the ability of imagining alternatives is debilitated by the absence of accountability and the slow and incessant wearing out of bodies, desires, aspirations, and possibilities? How can imagination thrive in this landscape of death and artificial immobility? How have artists and writers imagined and narrated this Mediterranean and its legacies of empire?

These "opacities" demand places in which we can listen together to the traces of a Mediterranean visuality that echoes the multiple stories and perspectives, the contradictions and dissonances of a story yet to be narrated. A poetic language which discloses but also protects that which is being imagined; a "poethic"—in the sense of "a complex form of realism" which doesn't simply explore "art's significance as a form of living in the real world," but it's an ethos. And the ethos that animates many of the works discussed in the book is one of bearing witness to the contradictions that the psych-affective responses of the protagonists to this "magical" atmosphere of violence make legible.

In his important contribution and rereading of Fanon, Nouri Gana writes that, in Arab cultural representation, the psycho-affective response of the occupation makes legible a series of contradictions, or what he describes as "the unsuspecting divides between speech and praxis, illness and insight, suicide and protest, grief and grievance, defeat and defiance, compliance and critique,

8 *Imagination Besieged*

creativity and stasis, commitment and detachment."[21] As we shall see in the book, the protagonists of these stories experience emotions and feelings that are often distorted by the realities of oppression that take agency away from them. They are not hopeful characters, but neither do they surrender to their alienation and sense of powerlessness.

For the context of this study, the case of Palestine proves an important example of the ways in which settler colonialism imposes its oppressive realities that are meant to debilitate, physically and mentally, and wear out the Palestinian population. How do the poet and storyteller navigate this fragmented landscape? How does the poet craft her language to tell her story when words are deadly, dead, colourless knickknacks and demand accountability? The sense of alienation and fragmentation, which often pervents the reconstruction of a sense of community and wholeness is addressed by Palestinian artists and writers in their works. The protagonist of Adania Shibli's *Minor Detail*, a journalist from Ramallah, attempts the difficult and dangerous journey across the fragmented and controlled landscape of Palestine to gather information on the case of a young Bedouin woman murdered by the IDF in the late '40s. She wants to retell the story from the young woman's perspective. But her attempt is destined to fail. As the journey becomes more dangerous, it also becomes more evident that the narrative of the truth is owned by the occupiers.

Shibli's novel asks question of the kind of language that can counteract the violence of the language of the occupation, and by acknowledging the impossibility to escape this violence, it turns towards the language of "minor details." She observes and describes details that almost seem to make no sense, compared to the monstrosity of the rape and murder of the young woman. She makes tangible the tension at the heart of Palestinian's experience between the deadly implications of the occupation on Palestinian sense of freedom and the aspirations for national liberation and more simply the affirmation of life in the face of so much brutality.

Through speculative fiction, documentary practices, and poetry, the works discussed in the book find in poetic language a way of witnessing the realities and histories of violence that have as their imagined and real geography, the Mediterranean. The authors discuss and problematise the violence of language and of the archives and the limitations of the ways of seeing we have inherited from the hegemonic apparatuses of knowledge.

The works listen to and write in the gaps opened by the silences of hegemonic narratives. They record the barely visible, audible; the voice in the noise, what has been removed, is absent, or has already died. They investigate the aftermath of crisis and destruction and pose questions about witnessing and testimony, reliable and unreliable narrators; about truth and its obfuscation, what is "real" and what is "fiction"; what is considered "legal" and the subtle line that separates it from what is deemed "illegal." They pose questions of ethical responsibility and poetic justice. Whether my own account of the mysterious disappearance of Angela or the stories narrated by Etel Adnan, Corrado

Like Stubborn Fires 9

Alvaro, Shuruq Harb, Jessika Khazrik, Adania Shibli, and Mahdi Fleifel, these acts of storytelling are ways of preparing for a future in which we might achieve accountability for the impunity of the violence and the crimes committed. This demand for accountability, for instance, drives Jessika Khazrik's multipart research and poem *Mount Mound Refuse*, in which the artist speculates on the "dead-deal," which brought mountains of toxic waste from Italy to be dumped in several sites in and around Beirut, and denounces the human and environmental cost of this deadly deal and its toxic legacies.

How to deal with a situation in which what is false has become truth, and conversely, the truth is being framed as false witnessing? What is the role of art but to unsettle and problematise those given truths and ways of seeing? The story of the "Poison Ships," how I have renamed them, and which is discussed in Chapter 7, is relevant here because every effort was made to silence its witnesses and the truth about the large international network that linked states, private companies, and criminal organisations across the Mediterranean around the business of waste disposal. If information and evidence have been obfuscated, Khazrik's poem insists on asking questions and unearthing fragments of the story, wondering whether imagination can open a space for justice.

Similarly, in her novel *Sitt Marie Rose,* discussed in Chapter 5, Adnan asks whether the memories of violence and the scars of the civil war can be healed, and whether in retelling those stories of violence, the poet might be able to do justice to the memory of the young Marie, a woman from the Christian community who had decided to dedicate her life to support the Palestinian cause and will be punished for her "betrayal" of the community during the civil war. Based on real events, the novel looks at the civil war through the disquieted eyes of this young woman, who cannot comprehend war's violence and brutality. Marie had refused the sectarianism and a narrow definition of ethnic-identity. Adnan's novel sheds light on the cruelty and the colonial legacy of the civil war, but more importantly, on the woman's defiance in the face of this absurd violence. Her retelling is a way of reframing the protagonist's story in a way that makes it possible to imagine cross-Mediterranean solidarities among women who, in their differences, are exposed to similar degrees and levels of brutality and degradation.

Witnessing the realities of Arab asylum seekers travelling to Europe brings Palestinian Danish film-maker Madhi Fleifel face-to-face with the social and economic collapse, which links together the lives of both asylum seekers and poor and disenfranchised Greeks. In his short-documentary *Xenos*, Madhi Fleifel witnesses the human tragedy of a group of Palestinian refugees from Lebanon in Athens through the story told by one of the three, Abu Eyad. In dialogue with Fleifel, in a moment of despair, the man is heard saying, "this country kills your soul." Both those who have left and those who stayed seem to be linked by a common destiny: living under a state of physical, emotional, and cognitive "siege," between instability and survival, need and stasis. If

10 *Imagination Besieged*

addiction becomes a form of "escape" from the prison that Athens "feels" like to the three Palestinian men, for those who remain and are stuck with the realities of an apartheid regime, the fragmentation, control over the territory, and the lives of the Palestinians, escape too might become a way to deal with the debilitating realities of the occupation.

But again, "escape" might not be the exact term to describe the range of emotional responses triggered by the state of debilitation engineered by the occupation. Love, pain, desire, disappointment, and aspirations are distorted by the violence of settler colonialism. These distortions also mean that coloniser and colonised do not live, exist in, or perceive the same realities; the meaning that "freedom," "alienation," and "escape" acquire completely shift depending on which perspective one is looking at and speaking from.

In two video works discussed in Chapter 8, artist Shuruq Harb reflects on the sense of entrapment and alienation experienced by Palestinians who are forced to grapple and find ways to survive these fragmented and split realities. Within this impossibility to live their lives freely, the protagonists of Harb's short films *The White Elephant (2018)* and The *Jump* (2021) enact small and almost undetectable acts of refusal and resistance that seem to offer, if only briefly and for a very limited time, moments of freedom. But this "freedom" is framed by the realities of the occupation and is shaped by them, in its most debilitating effects. In her *The Right to Maim*,[22] Jasbir Puar observes how the occupation not only uses checkpoints, divided highways, and illegal settlements to fragment the Palestinian's landscape but also targets young people on their knees, creating "infrastructural impediment to deliberately inhibit and prohibit movement," as well as, as Harb's video highlights, their mental health. The mental and physical effects of experiences of war and continuous violence of the occupation are the most obvious manifestation of what Puar calls "the right to maim," that is, "the infliction of injury and the maintenance of a perpetually debilitated, but living, Palestinian population under Israeli control."[23]

In *The Jump*, two women express their opinion of why someone might choose to die by jumping. "Jumping is like an adventure," one of the two women says. "I understand it. If someone wants to die without fear, jumping is a fun experience … so one dies happy … euphoria makes one forget where one is heading to." Sitting by the swimming pool, one of the two women observes that it's important to find ways of being outside the oppressive eye of the occupation and be able to express oneself freely. In water, she states, one finds a space where all obstacles put in the way by the occupation can be removed. Could this extreme act of "jumping" be understood in terms of a refusal to continue living when life has become impossible. Harb's works deal with the space opened by gestures of refusal in the face of the alienation Palestinians are forced to live with. In a sense, the protagonists of her stories enact their agency in the face of the impossibility to move and express themselves freely.

Like Stubborn Fires 11

The different stories have a common denominator: the refusal to move on and accept and condone the violence and suffering inflicted on individuals and entire communities by this politics of death. Instead, their storytelling is an attempt at exposing, problematising and denouncing the "obfuscations" that the present seeks to conceal, the ways in which the occupation (and we could add here the 'ndrangheta) wages a psychological warfare on those they seek to oppress, instilling fear and terror to control, render passive, and debilitate the ability to conduct a normal life, to come together as community, to mourn or celebrate, to freely express emotions, to *feel freely*, and imagine outside and free from the sense of being under a constant state of siege.

In the last chapter, Movements at Sea (Annotations on "Off You Paper Trail," 2024), I discuss the collaboration between artist Shuruq Harb and myself which led to the making of short experimental short film "Off You Shore. Paper Trail" (2024), set within the Liberty Hellas Museum, once a "Liberty ship" turned commercial boat today hosting a floating museum at the port of Piraeus in Athens. The Liberty ship became a catalyst for the complex relation to the Mediterranean basin which Harb and I shared, and for a dialogue about movement and accessibility. The Liberty ship carries memories of hope and despair relating to narratives of return and becomes a haunting vessel. Following the eerie demise of these ships, which often undertook tragically fated journeys, the short film comes to terms with the inherent contradictions of archiving and what resists such preservation, to engage with the unspoken, unrecorded histories and subversive ways of movement of people and goods.

Drawing on the critical insights by maritime historian Gelina Harlaftis, who studied Onassis' offshore innovative model in the shipping business, and on historian Vanessa Ogle, who has argued for an understanding of decolonisation as also "a financial event," in this last chapter, I reflect on how the intangibility of power is rendered in aesthetic and poetic choices which attempt to capture the atmosphere of secrecy. "Off You Shore. Paper Trail," like the other works discussed here, adopts "diversion" as a technique to find an "elsewhere" from which to analyse and speak of the obfuscations of information and obstacles that Harb and I encountered in accessing information about the relationship between offshore, shipping, and the demise of nationalism.

In this book, somewhere between the sense of alienation and the desire for freedom, we witness the stubborn fire, as Darwish might have called it, that animates those who are made to live with the ruins of a "toxic" present. In their actions, in their defiance of the given rules and codes that "identify" their respective communities, in the violence that has been unleashed against them, we glimpse the sparks of the fires of refusal, which is also the legacy of their lives and stories. Retelling and recomposing those truths that the archive of the Mediterranean throws ashore is but an attempt by many of the authors to bear witness to the divisions and schisms that European modernity has produced by obfuscating possible alternative modernities and reframe what

12 *Imagination Besieged*

could have been, but also what unfinished future potentials those stories point towards.

Simone Weil once wrote that "we must not weep so that we may not be comforted" and thus gets used to "intolerable"[24] human misery and suffering. Through this act of witnessing the effects on human life of histories of violence, in witnessing the absences, gaps, and silences of historical archives and hegemonic narratives, their works refuse precisely this act of mourning. The refusal to mourn, which is a constant in the stories and essays in the book, is the storyteller's form of resistance against normalisation of human loss and suffering. Despite the great loss and pain the stories tell, they articulate and give voice to something that is less than hope but subtler than despair. It's certainly not resignation. It's the stubbornness of the protagonists' refusal of their dehumanisation, the stubbornness of the authors in telling and retelling those stories, in not accepting to "move on." The works discussed express something that cannot really be described as hopefulness towards the future. It is more the awareness of the inevitability of change. And a persistent, stubborn insistence with which the protagonists, their stories, acts, and ideas, even after their deaths, continue to live and insist on living in the memories and the new stories they inspire. This is perhaps their most radical refusal, their stubborn insistence on not dying.

Notes

1 In *Memory of Forgetfulness* Mahmoud Darwish writes, "And when they set about putting the siege under siege, did they know that in bringing the actual out of the marvelous into the ordinary they were supplanting the legend and revealing to the misguided Prophet of Doom the secrets of a heroism woven by the movement from the self-evident to the self-evident? As if a handful of human beings were to rebel against the order of things so that this people, whose birth was tempered with stubborn fire, should not be made equal to a flock of sheep herded over the fence of complicity by the Shepherds of Oppression in collusion with the Guardian of the Legend." Mahmoud Darwish, *Memory for Forgetfulness* (Beirut August 1982: University of California Press, 2013), 25.

2 Éduard Glissant, *Caribbean Discourse: Selected Essays* (Charlottesville: University of Virginia Press, 1989), 20.

3 Ann Laura Stoler, "Imperial Debris. On Ruins and Ruination," *CULTURAL ANTHROPOLOGY*, 23(2), 191–219, 194, 2008.

4 See Vito Teti, *Terra Inquieta* (Rubettino Editore, 2016). All translations of Vito Teti are mine, unless specified.

5 As Michael Rothberg writes in *The Implicated Subject. Beyond Victims and Perpetrators* (Stanford University Press, 2019).

"Derived from the Latin stem *implicāre*, meaning to entangle, involve, or connect closely, 'implication,' like the proximate but not identical term 'complicity,' draws attention to how we are 'folded into' (im-pli-cated in) events that at first seem beyond our agency as individual subjects. [...] 'Implicated subjects occupy positions aligned with power and privilege without being themselves direct agents of harm; they contribute to, inhabit, inherit, or benefit from regimes of domination but do not originate or control such regimes.' An implicated subject is neither a victim nor a

Like Stubborn Fires 13

perpetrator, but rather a participant in histories and social formations that generate the positions of victim and perpetrator, and yet in which most people do not occupy such clear-cut roles." Rothberg, M., "Feeling Implicated: An Introduction," *Parallax*, *29*(3), 265–281, 2023.

6 I could perhaps describe my approach as partly "auto-ethnographic" in the sense that, "it articulates the intersection of cognitive and somatic experience. Through narrative craft, it stories a life lived, and in so doing, engages theory to make sense of how that life is socio-historically situated. It demonstrates the systemic consequences on everyday interactions, while simultaneously showing how a constellation of interactions both sustain and change those very systems." From Sandra L. Pensoneau-Conway, "Autoethnography: Storied Scholarship," *International Encyclopedia of Education*, edited by Robert J Tierney, Fazal Rizvi, Kadriye Ercikan; Fourth edition (Elsevier, 2023), 102–106. See also, Elizabeth Ettorre, *Autoethnography as Feminist Method. Sensitising the feminist 'I'* (Routledge, 2017).

7 Corrado Alvaro, C., *Gente in Aspromonte*, pres. e note di M. Pomilio, Garzanti, Milano. 1982 [1930]; Corrado Alvaro, *Calabria*, Nemi, Firenze; n. ed. con pref. di L. Bigiaretti e un saggio di D. Scafoglio, Qualecultura Jaca Book, Vibo Valentia 1990. Alvaro, C. 1990b, *Ritratto di Melusina*, in Id., *L'amata alla finestra* 1929; ed. completa (1953), in Alvaro 1999a. Corrado Alvaro, *Un treno nel Sud* (1958), introduzione di V. Teti, n. ed. Rubbettino, Soveria Mannelli 2017. All translations of Alvaro's excerpts in the book are mine.

8 Vito Teti, *Terra inquieta. Per un'antropologia dell'erranza meridionale*, Rubbettino, Soveria, Mannelli, 2015. *Quel che resta. L'Italia dei paesi, tra abbandono e ritorno*, Donzelli, 2017. *Il vampiro e la melanconia*, Donzelli, 2018. "Mediterraneum. Geografie dell'interno" in G. Cacciatore, M. Signore et al., *Mediterraneo e cultura europea*, Rubbettino, Soveria Mannelli, 2003, pp. 107–128. Teti, *Luoghi, culti, memorie dell'acqua*, in Teti V. (a cura di), 2003; *Il senso dei luoghi. Memoria e vita dei paesi abbandonati*, pref. di P. Matvejevic, Roma, Donzelli (n. ed. aggiornata, ivi, 2014). *Tradizione e modernità nell'opera di Corrado Alvaro*, in A. M. Morace (a cura di), *Corrado Alvaro e la letteratura tra le due guerre*, Pellegrini, Cosenza, 2005: 515–540. *I luoghi e i disastri. Le reti della storia, della natura e degli individui*, in Guidoboni, E. Valensise, G., *L'Italia dei disastri dati e riflessioni sull'impatto degli eventi naturali 1861–2013* (Bologna: Bononia University Press), 359–373.

9 Claudio Fogu, "We Have Made the Mediterranean; Now We Must Make Mediterraneans," in *Critically Mediterranean: Temporalities, Aesthetics, and Deployments of a Sea in Crisis*, edited by yasser elhariry and Edwige Tamalet Talbayev (Cham: Springer, 2018), 181–197.

10 Franz Fanon, "Concerning Violence," in *The Wretched of the Earth*, 1961, p. 4.

11 Tina Campt, "Black Visuality and the Practice of Refusal," *Women and Performance Journal*, February 2019. Available through: https://www.womenandperformance.org/ampersand/29-1/campt

12 Raffaella A. Del Sarto, Sectarian Securitization in the Middle East and the Case of Israel, *International Affairs*, *97*(3), 759–778, (May 2021).

13 Predrag Matvejevic, *Mediterranean. A Cultural Landscape* (University of California Press, 1999), 12.

14 Iain Chambers, "A Fluid Archive," 2019. Available through: https://mediterraneanblues.blog/wp-content/uploads/2019/08/a_fluid_archive.pdf.pdf

15 Iain Chambers, "What is 'Black' in the Black Mediterranean?" Available through: https://postcolonialpolitics.org/what-is-the-black-in-the-black-mediterranean/

16 Iain Chambrs, *Thinking with the Diver. The Mediterranean in Historical Perspective* (The British Academy Library, 2020). Available through: https://www.thebritishacademy.ac.uk/documents/910/JBA-8s1-02-Chambers.pdf

14　*Imagination Besieged*

17 Saidiya Hartman, "The Anarchy of Colored Girls Assembled in a Riotous Manner," *South Atlantic Quarterly*, *117*, 465–490, 486, (July, 2018).

18 Nouri Gana, *Melancholy Acts: Defeat and Cultural Critique in the Arab World* (New York, NY, 2023; online edn., Fordham Scholarship Online, 18 Jan. 2024), 18.

19 Gana, *Melancholy Acts*, p. 18.

20 Aurde Lorde, "The Uses of Anger: Women Respond to Racism," *Sister/Outsider: Essays and Speeches* (Freedom, CA: The Crossing Press, 1984).

21 Gana, *Melancholy Acts*, p. 4.

22 Jasbir K. Puar, *The Right to Maim: Debility, Capacity, Disability* (Durham, N.C.: Duke University Press, 2017).

23 Puar, *The Right to Maim*, p. X.

24 Simone Weil, *Gravity and Grace*, translated by Emma Crawford and Mario von der Ruhr (London: Routledge, 2002), 14.

1 *Sciarra* (After Angela) I

Shar, sciarra. It all made sense when you told me that our languages have the evil of two worlds in them. My tongue knows it, when *sciarra* would make it drum in thirsty mouths. *Sciarra*, setting your face on fire. *Sciarra*, a trumpet announcing their arrival: walking dead, with shepherd tools, gelatine in their hair, thick hands, guns, and their empty eyes. Don't get in trouble, you say. They are looking for *sciarria*. They're looking for a reason to have a fight. For the evil to come out and possess them. They try to tame its burning fire. But they fail and fail miserably. All is burning: the mountains, the coast, the sea, the cars, the animals, the beautiful Aspromonte, the houses, the people, the hearts, the desires, and the future, already consumed, that never comes.

Sciarra, I said. Who brought evil and death to your door? Who stole your smile? Who gave you the kiss of death? Who made you into a beautiful, melancholic flower? Some say punishment was the adequate response to a race of criminals. Others say it's because of the trembling earth, this demonic ground. We are demons lost in this land without hope.

DOI: 10.4324/9781003492634-2

16 *Imagination Besieged*

Who can afford to be "angry"?
The poet asks.
Anger, a luxury not everyone can afford.
In this economy of loss,
rebuts the feminist critic,
anger is incalculable debt.
the bad debt
that cannot
and will not
be repaid.
it will be excessive,
unconsolidated,
debt broken
from credit.
Anger is a broken soul,
A song,
A battle cry.
It is hope pinned down to the ground
—it screams you might be killing,
motherfucker,
but you won't kill
this
is
a virus.
You won't stop
the flood
streaming
through
this open
incalculable
wound.

Sciarra *(After Angela) I* 17

Calm fell on the quiet and peaceful landscape of wild chestnuts and olive trees, where the goat and the wolf play hide and seek. Silence fell on your disappearance. Silence, on the shameful event. Silence, on your violated body, silently slipping into oblivion.

At the end of a long day, your callous hands dropped down, tired by so much work. You were made of the rocks of Aspromonte. the White Montain. For the local, the bitter Mount—bitter like lemon juice, freshly squeezed; like the tears you swallow in silence. Bitter like bitter daisies; like the taste of salt and goat milk; like the dandelions you boiled and offered me to cure this melancholic, restless soul. Bitter like the tears we never shed, like the smell of muriatic acid, like your decomposing body, feeding the wolf, humus for the forest.

They took your body, your life, and your dignity. They stole and cheated on the future and the hope of entire generations. And the poet wrote, "there is no defect or convention that eventually, in a corrupt society, does not become a virtue."[1]

18 *Imagination Besieged*

Aspromonte. Aspros. ضَيِّأ.
But never pure or candid.
White as in bitter
Bitter like the taste of a plumb off season.
Like the season of kidnappings.
The reason for this
being your sharp edges,
the upsurging force
the deadly cliffs
and the shifting ground
that spelt out disasters.
Aspro like the impervious ways
through which shepherds
took their sheep
to die in the fire.
Aspromonte:
"Violence rises from every square meter
as if from a metallic forest."[2]
Aspromonte. A land of oblivion
constantly remembered.
Aspromonte. The litany of laments
the women performed
for three days and nights,
dancing, singing songs to you
Aspromonte. They took your life
one day, because it was worth more
than the eternity of a marriage
which carried you away,
down the cliff.
You fell,
blood all around.
The brain gashing out.
Aspros, but also brown, grey and dark red,
Stained with blood,
the soil,
the bitter taste of salt,
and lemon juice
burning my lips
until there was no words
left to described it.

Sciarra *(After Angela) I*   19

What if there is no way back home? You say. And I told you the stories of the many Ulysses who never made it back home. Because Ulysses is a story of departures from "a land without promise, in a land without return."[3] You never returned; did not leave, did not stay, and did not arrive. Where did you go that night? Did you drive to their place? Did they come to find you? Did they wake you up? How many were they? Did you know them? Where did they take you? Did they blindfold you? Did they take you to the fields? Did they hurt you? Did they hit your head? Did they shoot you in the heart? What did they do with your young body? Did they give it to the dogs or the pigs? Did they dissolve it in acid? Did they use your love to destroy you, destroy us all? "Who are you looking for?" He wants to know, by which he meant to say, "Who do you belong to?" You, who were born in this ungrateful land.

You left one day, left this world to never return.

Until your eyes closed and time stopped, and you were free from the guilt and the burden of having been born in this land without promise, in a land of no return.

20 *Imagination Besieged*

It remains that bowing is a complacent and interested form of relationship with power that runs through the entire Calabrian society, with the special responsibility of those who have sold off their intelligence, their professionalism, their freedom, waiting for favors, only to grumble in silence.... It didn't help. Calabria, in this atmosphere of perpetual crisis, because of the fragility of its economic and social fabric, risks drowning and dying for the too many acts of bowing, which define differently all the social classes.[4]

To bow, to bend your knee, to twist and turn, to loop, deviate, and change course. You move your head up and down to show agreement, approval, to signal the message has been received. Nodding is like a note of encouragement. It creates an atmosphere in which nodding theatrically reinstates the order of things. They say it's the way it is. They say nothing will ever change, and then look away. They don't want to see. They say run, or it will catch up with you. They say you will become bitter. You will be swallowed by apathy and oblivion, which are sticky like delicious chestnut honey. There is no space for dreams or changes. They say don't come back, forget about us, our bodies and aspirations bent and withered by the *scirocco*.

They repeat you had choices, and the best choice was to stay away, never tell, never return. As if you and I had an option or a say. As if we could decide whether we wanted to become witnesses of the same old lie. Nodding, like bowing, Sara Ahmed once said, is a form of recognition that implies that the problem is safely constructed as being somewhere else. It can be a way of not recognising one's implication in a problem at the very moment that the problem is recognised. *A nod can be how a problem is enacted by the appearance of being heard.*[5] And so, by bowing we accept.

I was 12 years old when I witnessed how you give a "lesson" and set an "example" and leave an "impression" on a young mind. Fear and intimidation. It was in the middle of our Italian literature class that a small man in his 50s, with big callous hands and a jovial face, came one morning after his son had received a complaint note from the school. He walked in, apologised for interrupting the lesson, and in his Calabrian-inflected accent asked his son to stand up. The young boy stood, and hesitantly walked towards the teacher's desk with a face which knew already what to expect. A fist started hitting the young boy on his face and head, multiple times, each time harder, until the confused teacher intervened.

Humiliation is a technology of coercion and control. The silence that followed the senseless aggression was full of questions to which the answer was an embarrassed and loaded silence. No one explained to us, kids, why it was so vital to always remain discreet, obedient, and especially mind our businesses; why it was important to avoid certain places—why the sea, but not the mountain. We were just 12 years old. Twelve, the same years my schoolmate spent in jail. For him, as for many youths, inside or outside, it is equally like living in a self-imposed exile.

the sound of rusted metal
rubbing against
the skin of time.

Sciarra *(After Angela) I*   23

There is no rest
for those who cannot live
Only the smell of
burnt gasoline
to keep company,
the endless lies
to remain alert
to stay safe
to remain sane
move with the tides
above the grave
they dig for you.
Those who want
to bury you alive
with their idea of nation-state,
returning or staying?
No one gets to choose,
you say,
there is no way back,
no promised place.

I will never know if the look in your eyes was
anger or grief,
a path of destruction or liberation,
but I tried to hold them both gently.

Sciarra *(After Angela) I*   25

Silence interrupted by the sound
anger makes when it hits the tone,
and the feet stomps the ground.
Anger is music extracted from
the noise of "everything goes".
That's why the poem cannot
been delivered
without anger,
only *in* and *within*
and *with* the music,
that is anger
inviting us to listen
in-between the lines
in the emotional nuances
and undertones.

Anger-in-excess is hope,
refusing to succumb,
is the movement
of bodies to the tune.

dancing,
clapping,
shouting,
swinging,

It is the sound of collapse.
Violence is also a dance.
And we dance
so we can unforget
we dance so we can survive death.

And our dance is
a coded language,
a poem whispered
in-between
the walls
of this prison.

And we dance
we dance
And escape from it
by dancing together.

Notes

1 Corrado Alvaro, *il nostro tempo e la speranza.*
2 From Etel Adnan, *Sitt Marie Rose*, p. 13.
3 This phrase is borrowed from Ali Ahmad Sa'id's poem Ulysses.
4 Excerpt from: Vito Teti. "Terra inquieta (Italian Edition)" 2018, translation mine.
5 Sara Ahmed, "Nodding as a non-performative". Available through: https://feministkilljoys.com/2019/04/29/nodding-as-a-non-performative/

2 *Sciarra* (After Angela) II

Angela Bueti, my great-grandaunt, disappeared one night in 1977 in Melia di Scilla, a small village on the slopes surrounding the Aspromonte Forest in the region of Calabria, Southern Italy. At the time of her disappearance, she was 49. Born into a family of farmers, the last of seven kids, like all the men and women of her family, she worked in the fields all day long, and when the work was over, as an unmarried woman, she devotedly took care of her old parents.

I never met her, and the only trace of her existence is an old, faded black and white photograph in which she appears at a festive occasion. She dresses black, as it was costumery at that time. She stands next to her parents, my great-grandfather and great-grandmother. She looks proud and merry. I recognise some familiar features: her large forehead, the gentle chin, and the jovial face of the Buetis. But she also seems to shy away from the intrusive gaze of the camera, as if a photo could steal her soul. Angela is not only my grandaunt but also, as I will argue, in many ways, she embodies a region and its destiny, connected to the histories of violence and their impacts on people's everyday lives. It is the point of departure for other stories of everyday life of common people who like hers, have been muted, rendered invisible. For me, Angela became the embodiment of the dramatic destiny of a region stuck in the aftermath of endless crisis, violence, and social collapse.

To gain access to any document or information about her disappearance in the archives of the Reggio Calabria judicial court has proven impossible. I never received any answers to the many enquiries. Silence. The inaccessibility of the archive feels a bit like a conspiration between 'ndrangheta and the State in the management of realities and information. Many of my questions are about what happened to her that day or night when she disappeared, what are the reasons and the motives of her disappearance, and who knew and preferred to remain silent? These questions will have to remain unanswered. And I made peace with the fact this is a story full of gaps and missing parts. But how to tell a story made of gaps? None of my close relatives, who are still alive, has a clear memory of her. My father recalls a phone call he had with my grandmother, who at the time was undergoing breast cancer therapy, in which she informed him of a violent argument she had with my grandfather's

DOI: 10.4324/9781003492634-3

28 *Imagination Besieged*

brother-in-law. She said he had harassed the young woman. My grandmother didn't hesitate to confront the man. The phone call ended, and sometime later Angela disappeared.

The disappearance of Angela has become a kind of obsession. But I gave up the idea of solving the mystery of her disappearance, or of piecing together the missing information of her murder. Angela's disappearance is like a shadow casted on this paradise inhabited by devils. And it is this shadow that I wish to summon and ask questions to. Angela's is the story of a double violence—that of patriarchal culture and a criminal mentality. Of a Calabrian peasant who, despite the larger social transformation of the country, became one of the many victims of an absurd and brutal violence perpetuated, as it often happens here, by people she most likely knew. She share her destiny with Maria Chindamo, Barbara Corvi, Simona Napoli, Lea Garofalo, Maria Concetta Cacciola, Giuseppina Pesce, and Denise Cosco, some of the women who have been punished for having refused and rejected familial ties and belonging, or for simply having had contact with someone affiliated with the criminal organisation known as 'ndrangheta.

In her study of women's lives in the context of 'ndrangheta, sociologist Sabrina Garofalo observes that "family control becomes social control," not only through the physical proximity of the family but also and very much so through a capillary system of relations and belonging that extends, through a system of "comparaggi," way beyond the family. A network of support, but also of mutual control. Women thus are controlled and denied their process of subjectivation; their lives and bodies do not belong to them but are a community's affair, a "collective domestication"[1] of bodies and affects.

A control that justifies the dishonour, the punishment for the simple fact of having challenged or placed themselves in antagonism to male power. This is the case of Lea Garofalo, who had decided to collaborate on a police investigation and revealed the details of a bloody civil war between two 'Ndrangheta families that left 40 dead. Lea Garofalo, 35, was lured to Milan in 2009 by members of the Calabrian 'Ndrangheta—among them her ex-partner and father of her daughter—before being tortured, shot dead, and dumped in 50 litres of acid at a rural warehouse. The court said that members of the gang watched the acid vat for three days to ensure Garofalo's corpse had totally dissolved.[2]

These disappearances speak volumes of the kind of violent environment that defines women's life and death in Calabria. Angela was "just" an unmarried woman and a peasant—and her life, outside the reproductive function, was worth less than that of a cow. This is what my uncle keeps repeating: the police did not investigate the case further because of her sex and humble origins. In rural villages in Calabria at that time for a woman to be single meant that, if the father or brothers were not around to "protect" her honour, a woman could be treated like a thing, an animal. Customary expressions and sexist jokes disclose the type of objectification women were subjected to. *A fimmana senza statu è comu 'u pani senza lavatu* (A woman without matrimonial status is like bread without yeast), or *Scecchi e fimmini, vastunati nca aggrizzanu* (Donkeys and women, beatings that get lost), or again, *A fimmina a vint'anni o a mariti o a scanni* (A woman at the age of 20, either you marry her or you kill her). In all, a "fimmina" must be dominated or punished.

At the time of my grandaunt disappearance, writer and educator Augusta Frisina wrote a report published with the title "Donne alla sbarra" [Women on the stand] (1979), on the difficult conditions of Calabrian women, who lived, she observed, "in a universe and a world which have been betrayed, abandoned and relegated to be 'our colony at home."[3] Compared to their "sisters" in other regions, the report observes, women in Calabria were subjected to a double oppression—that of a traditionally patriarchal society relegated to their traditional reproductive in the household and "objects" of possession, too often becoming the subject of violence and unwanted for attentions—and the semi-colonial living and working conditions, under the supervision of barons, middlemen, and greedy and cruel landowners. Calabria was effectively a "colony at home," exploited economically but abandoned socially, without infrastructure or education.

Frisina writes that violence against women is "difficult to unpick and condemn, because masked as marital contract, legitimated in a society that believes and delivers a phony exaltation of motherhood, which celebrates Mother Day, that is moved by the cult of the mother, that cries and wipes and cheats on women." First wife and mother and then, if anything, worker, refuge of the family, and angels of the home. The dominant sentiment was that if women were murdered or raped, they deserved it, as they must had done something wrong, indecent, inappropriate, and shameful.

Availed by the Codice Rocco[4] (from the surname of the fascist minister who signed it), a woman could be killed by her partner if accused of infidelity, or she could be raped and the men would go unpunished by "reparatory marriage," de facto denying any accountability and form of justice for the victims. It was "normal" to think that if a woman had mysteriously disappeared or murdered, she must have done something wrong. So, I guess I should believe that Angela had done something wrong to deserve her destiny, like Roberta Lanzino, whose lifeless body was found in the mountains of Falconara Albanese, in 1998, undressed and covered in brushwood in a field not far from where her scooter was found. She was tortured, sexually raped, stabbed, and suffocated with the shoulder straps of her shirt stuffed into her mouth.[5] Traces of seminal fluid were found on the body. But the perpetrators were never found. What wrong could this young girl possibly have done? Mary Cirillo too was killed by her partner in Monasterace Marina, simply because she had decided to live her life autonomously and away from her partner's abuses. I must believe that it was the appropriate punishment for having dared to cross the line, to raise their head, and refuse to bow.

30 *Imagination Besieged*

Did she betray her community? Was it her crime to have spoken in the face of some unnameable secret? Was her fault to have fallen in love with the wrong man? Did she refuse the Law? I must learn from this "example" and "exemplary" punishment to not dare to cross the line again. Alessandra Dino writes about violence in the context of 'Ndrangheta, that it "creates bonds and relationships [...] symbolic showcase of power, tool to demarcate the boundaries of belonging and legitimacy. But it expands also to the quotidian, crossing the sphere of emotions and the most relevant questions of the 'Ndrangheta identity: secrecy and power, death, fear, pain, culpability, repentance, honour and shame."[6]

Violence is pervasive, and it is simultaneously public (control and isolation of women) and private (in the household). In her testimony, Giuseppina Pesce, says that her husband "was beating me up because I was rebelling, because I said what I thought, and in order to silence me, he used to become very aggressive." The modalities of the murder of Lea Garofalo and others, are peculiar in the sense that 'ndrangheta always makes sure to leave no traces, but it also wants to make sure to render their deeds invisible. The way in which many of these women were murdered, by dissolving their bodies in muriatic acid, is symbolic of the desire to literally silence and corrode their "dangerous" words.

In this context, feminicide is used as a "punishment" for the injury to the honour either of the family or of the community. It is a way of regulating community life and perpetuating 'ndrangheta power. Rebellion requires the annihilation of the rebel subjectivity: Lea Garofalo, Maria Concetta Caccciola, Tita Buccafusca, Angela Costantino, Barbara Corvi, Gelsomina Verde, who was tortured and killed at the age of 22 in Naples, and Rossella Casini. Women's experience within the context of 'ndrangheta is linked to the violation of their rights as women, to their continuous humiliation and chagrin. As Garofalo observes, "push [women's] subjectivities to the point of annihilation of themselves which gradually brings to a sense of resignation,"[7] and a feeling of impossibility to change their destiny, forced to live with fear and under constant scrutiny. 'Ndrangheta normalises violence, and Garofalo writes, "is fully involved in the construction of common sense, understood as a tool to maintain and define relationships, and that becomes 'normal' in the specific patriarchal culture of 'ndrangheta."[8]

Angela's disappearance was a message sent to my family. Like the one sent year laters, in 1991, to my father, and sprayed on the walls of what was to become our house, which said: "THIS WILL BECOME YOUR GRAVE." These kinds of intimidation are not uncommon in the everyday life of Calabrians—sometimes they translate into murderous realities; oftentimes they are meant to instil a sense of terror and suspiciousness, to establish physical and psychological control. Fear and devotion are sought after.

Anthropologist Vito Teti observes that the 'ndrangheta is not simply an organisation that seeks economic control but it also "interferes in emotions,

Sciarra *(After Angela) II* 31

and in this respect, the 'ndrangheta has the perverse ability, almost the dominion on affects, a sort of magical power." But one that has deeply toxic effects. The silence of the State archive speaks another kind of structural violence, that of erasure, of a legal system that is slow and incapacitated in its ability to adequately bring about justice and accountability. Structural inequities and corruption have created an institutional vacuum from within, meaning that Calabrians have always improvised their way of living amid continuous crisis, violence, corruption, and economic and social depression. People here live in resignation, for any form of social justice has failed to materialise.

In many cases, representatives of institutions have failed their communities without having been held accountable for those criminal acts; criminals are in and out of jail and are freely able, even from jail, to continue their business as usual. It is this lack of accountability that has developed into a sense of impossibility, incredulity, an atmosphere of mistrust, immobility, and resignation. For many people in my region, to put it simply, institutions have not cared—socially, politically, and economically—and thus cannot be trusted to deliver their many, too many, failed promises. But neither are their brigands and men of honour trustworthy, and their delivery of the promises, with their enormous logistic apparatus, comes at great expenses for the many. Calabrian society remains split, divided in its sense of belonging, disoriented, and at war with itself.

What kind of other life could have she lived? What kind of other stories could be told? Where the act of telling these stories is to participate in the construction of a collective memory of Calabria, one that acknowledges the impossibility to recuperate, or overcome the losses.

Notes

1 Sabrina Garofalo, *Donne, violenza e 'ndrangheta. Metodi, storie e politiche* (Novalogos, 2023), p. 61. All translations from Garofalo's book are mine.
2 "Italian mobester condemned by daughter's evidence," in *The Guardian* online, April 2012. Available through: https://www.theguardian.com/world/2012/apr/01/italian-mobster-jailed-by-daughters-evidence
3 Augusta Frisina, *Donne Alla Sbarra* (La Ginestra, 1979), p. 51. All translations are mine.
4 Penal Code, art. 587 "Whoever causes the death of his spouse, daughter or sister, in the act in which he discovers their illegitimate carnal relationship and in the state of anger determined by the offense caused to his or his family's honor, is punished with imprisonment from three to seven years. Anyone who, in the aforementioned circumstances, causes the death of a person who is in an illegitimate carnal relationship with their spouse, daughter or sister is subject to the same penalty. The art. 587 of the penal code therefore allowed the punishment to be reduced for anyone who killed his wife, husband, daughter or sister in order to defend "her or her family's honor." Codice Rocco in Enciclopedia Treccani. Available through: https://www.treccani.it/enciclopedia/delitto/#. Sara Musio, "L'elaborazione del Codice Rocco tra principi autoritari e continuità istituzionale" in ADIR-L'altro diritto, 1999. Available through: https://www.adir.unifi.it/rivista/1999/musio/cap1.htm.

32 *Imagination Besieged*

5 Available through: https://femminicidioitalia.info/caso/1988/luglio/27/roberta-lanzino-rende-miccisi-torremezzo-falconara-cosenza

6 Sabrina Garofalo, *Donne, violenza e 'ndrangheta. Metodi, storie e politiche* (Novalogos, 2023), p. 60.

7 Ibid, p. 64.

8 Ibid, p. 66.

3 Movement I: From Grief to Grievance

To acknowledge and embrace loss, Sarah Ahmed writes, is "to be willing to experience an intensification of the sadness that hopefulness postpones."[1] When the promise of happiness becomes the imperative to be happy and successful at all costs, obscuring the conditions and realities of living a capitalist life, feminists have not forgotten the sadness that comes from their experiences of loss; the invisibility of their condition as causalities of slow violence,[2] too often unseen and unaccounted for.

"To inherit feminism can mean to inherit sadness," continues Sarah Ahmed; a sadness that, however, does not become immobility. Rather, it might mean "holding on to things (including words) that are deemed sad by others. When words like 'racism' and 'sexism' are heard as melancholic, it is assumed we are holding on to something that has gone. So yes: we have to hold on as these histories are not gone." The insistence on remaining sad is the idea that we must "stay with the trouble," acknowledge but also very much work with and through what this "sadness" brings up. It is this impossibility to move on, to overcome loss in its present form, that is addressed in the works of the writers I discuss here.

If the disappearance of Angela Bueti is a loss that cannot be mourned because her body could not be buried and her soul given rest; if her disappearance is continuous, like the violence that has killed her and other women like her, then the sadness that comes from the consciousness of this impossibility, of this loss, is what propels an analysis of the materialities and conditions that produce a certain melancholic subjective predisposition, and to reflect on the political implications of this refusal to "move on." Simone Weil writes that "we must not weep so that we may not be comforted" and thus get used to "intolerable"[3] human misery and suffering. The refusal to mourn, in this sense, becomes a form of resistance against normalisation of human suffering.

In "Mourning and Melancholia,"[4] Freud observes how both mourning and melancholia are responses to the loss of something significant, whether that be a person or an ideal. However, while mourning can be brought to a gradual end, as the subject starts disinvesting from the lost object,

DOI: 10.4324/9781003492634-4

34 *Imagination Besieged*

melancholia, Freud argues, implies an attachment to the lost object that continues to haunt and inhabit the melancholic ego, in a way that can become pathological.

In *Coming to Writing*[5] (1972), Hélène Cixous rewrites mourning, melancholy, and loss as non-pathological an a life-affirming response, an initiation into the mysteries of life. Starting from her own experience, the displacement of her Jewish family, and especially the loss of her father, Cixous describes her initiation to writing as an experience of loss, as a generative void, a space that propels a different kind of way of seeing, of reading and writing, and a different ethical relationship with otherness. She turns to the poets of the Jewish diaspora—Clarice Lispector, Hetty Hillesum, and Paul Celan—who, as she observes, despite having witnessed and experienced the great loss, the despair and horror of historical violence, have turned this experience into a poetic gesture.

> But human beings try to live through the worst sufferings. To make humanity of them. To distil them, to understand their lesson. This is what the poets did in the concentration camps. And what we do ourselves, when the pain that strikes us in our personal life makes poets of us.[6]

If loss would seem to imply silence and muteness, in Cixous' reading, this loss produces whispers and laughter, dialogues, a poetic of relation which does not attempt to "kill the other," within and outside ourselves. Understanding the lesson of loss is what the poet does. Cixous insists on the generative dimension of life and its refusal to be contained, reduced to bare existence. Artistic expression becomes a way of being in conversation with the living and the dead, a way of refusing to succumb to the violence of denial, insisting on translating the experience of suffering into a poetic and life-affirming gesture.

Cixous argues for a form of militant writing capable of interrupting repressive poetic forms and de-pathologising affective responses to historical ruptures. Loss is at the centre of a short story by Calabrian writer and journalist Corrado Alvaro *Portrait of Melusina* (1929). In this story, loss has multiple dimensions: it is a loss of community, the end of an era, and the abandonment of entire villages; but also a much deeper form of loss, the lack of agency that both the young woman and her father are subjected to; the sense of loss "felt" by Melusina in seeing herself reflected and in part trapped in someone else's eyes and forms of representation.

Melusina is a young peasant from a village called La Rocca, in the heart of Aspromonte Forest, and her village, as the narrator tells us, had been abandoned due to natural catastrophes and migration. The church is unadorned, and even the dogs have decided to leave. Alvaro observes: "When Melusina stands on the doorstep, she appears to be the inhabitant of a world where men [sic.] have disappeared, and generations are about to become extinct."[7]

Movement I 35

The appearance of Melusina and her beauty stand in stark contrast to this desolate landscape of ruins.

A German painter, travelling across the region, sees the young woman, and impressed by her beauty wants to take a portrait. So, he asks the local Barons for permission, and Melusina's father, who had no choice in the face of this rather inappropriate request, accepts with scepticism and fear and asks the young woman to pose for this portrait. Once finished, Melusina refuses to look at it. She feels confused and violated by this foreigner man, and his presence became the sign of a bad omen.

Her reluctance to be portrayed is explained by Alvaro at the very beginning of the tale, in these words,

> I know that many Calabrian women have never had their portraits painted; it is enough to show up in one of our streets with a camera and all the women will turn their heads towards the wall; I only have a portrait of my mother, when she got married, and she is completely scared of finding herself in front of the camera once in her life, next to the groom standing in the act of protecting her. I say that I too suffer from this primordial restraint: I feel like I'm posing for something definitive before the mold of life breaks.[8]

Melusina wished someone had asked her what she desired and whether she felt okay with being portrayed. But, in this traditional Calabrian society in which peasants lived in a state of servitude, "no" was not a choice Melusina, or her father, were entitled to. Her beauty, we are told, becomes a "symbol of a life that has ended, of an abandoned tradition, of a dull and odorless nature."[9]

Melusina becomes a metaphor for a whole region, at a crossroad, in transition, living through the inevitable end of a traditional society, with its customs and cultural practices; and the advent of modernisation, which, almost in a prophetic way, the young woman, decries. As if to say that for this region, the process of modernisation arrived in the life of people like a catastrophe, a crisis of community life, tearing the social fabric apart, determining its symbolic death, and the fading away of ancient ties and relationships. But Alvaro is not nostalgic about the traditional world, where barons exploited their workers and women were relegated to their reproductive roles. He's more registering a transformation which left Calabrian society at great loss of identity, as communities were tore apart and had to reinvent themselves anew.

In this "world where men have disappeared," Melusina feels stuck and dislocated and thinks of her double, who will now travel to faraway places, with sadness. Alvaro observes the young peasant woman: "The secrets of the country's life are revealed in her, in her calm face with a low and straight forehead, as if compressed by a long weight borne on the head by a whole generation of women. (…) She, of course, in her low brow thinks, thinks of this double of

36   *Imagination Besieged*

herself who doesn't know where she is, and won't tell her man when she gets married: the only secret of her life, incomprehensible to herself."[10]

This sense of alienation that shatters and splits Melusina's self and identity mirrors the end of a world of traditional relationships and ways of living which had defined for millennials the survival of entire communities. Alvaro's story ends in the shadow of the old house, where we can hear Melusina "crying with the long, soft, calm cry of someone who is crying a death and will have to cry for a long time." Loss here becomes a crying voice, which, although lacking the words to express itself "properly," is in fact the expression of a melancholic subjectivity and of a language which sounds to many "a babbling," incomprehensible. Will Melusina be able to survive the changes? Or is her cry the expression of that hopeless future that awaits the region? And can Melusina cry be read as the expression of ancient grievances?

Alvaro sheds light on the lived violence experienced by many Calabrian women without necessarily offering a resolution or happy ending for his female characters, who live in a nightmare from which there seems to be no awakening. The Portrait of Melusina is the first in a collection entitled *L'amata alla finestra* [*The Beloved at the Window*] which narrates the stories of 33 characters, mostly women and witches who see things they keep silent about. What is interesting is that they see and sense a dramatic future that often eludes men. Melusina might not be an empowering tale, but, Alvaro, through his realism, offers a truthful and dignified reading of the "southern question." One that, without too much rhetoric, neither dismissing nor romanticising them, observes, describes, and reflects on the challenges, the prejudices, and difficulties and uncertainties that Calabrian people faced as modernisation determined the end of the traditional cultural practices, the crisis of identity.

The sadness that we hear in Melusina's calm and composed cry, after all, is no less rebellious than a loud shout. Melusina's sadness, her inconsolable cry, postpones the moment of hopefulness, since from where she stands, from the ruins of her village, imprisoned as she feels and is (both by her father, the landowner, and the painter's eyes and sense of ownership over her body), she's not granted the opportunity to "move on." She expresses a sadness that is neither hopeless nor hopeful, but somewhere in-between.

In *Melancholy Acts*, scholar Nouri Gani takes up the task of a decolonial re-reading of melancholy in the context of Arab cultural production and turns to the transformative dimension of Fanon's reading of melancholy, or as he describes it, the "generative movement from melancholizing to melancholicizing,"[11] the movement from the clinical and pathological to the analytical and political, which accords melancholy a political and revolutionary currency. For Gani, the passage from a pathological reading of melancholy, which relegates its subject to being "stuck" with loss, to an active and militant inhabitation of melancholy, is also a reminder of the decolonial dimension of affects. In this respect, melancholy is not simply

Movement I 37

read as an individual pathology, but as "a geopolitically differentiated and accented psychocultural dynamic that cuts through the personal and the political, the individual and the collective, the psychoaffective and the epistemological."[12]

Gani himself offers an example of what he describes as this conscious melancholicisation of certain events ("a laconic dramatization of the crucial swerve from settler colonial melancholization to decolonial melancholicization") in the lyrical epistolary short story "Letter from Gaza," written by Palestinian writer, poet, and PLO member Ghassan Kanafani, a contemporary of Fanon. The letter is addressed to a childhood friend, Mustafa, whom Kanafani is supposed to join in Sacramento, California. Both friends had dreamt of leaving Gaza and becoming rich, but while Mustafa jumped on the first opportunity and left for California, the speaker first moved to Kuwait to make enough money to pay for his trip. When the narrator goes back to Gaza from Kuwait to prepare for his imminent trip to California, the view of Gaza and the scenes of wreckage, misery, and desolation compel him to express his desire to leave, but when he goes to visit his 13-year-old niece, Nadia, in a Gaza hospital and sees her amputated leg, a realisation takes hold of him.

Nadia had lost her legs to protect her siblings from the bombs and flames. "Nadia could have saved herself. She could have run away and rescued her leg. But she didn't."[13] This encounter pushes the protagonist to stay and embrace the destiny of many Palestinians. Nadia unsettles, with her loss, the desire to escape, and compels the protagonist to revise his plan and reverse his commitment. Loss is here both in the amputated leg of the child and in Kanafani's loss of fear, and his decision to stay to fight for freedom and the liberation of Palestine.

Gani reads Kanafani's use of the epistolary form of the story as "[enacting] a chiastic reversal whose transformative and generative effect has the merit of a political epiphany"[14]: Nadia, whose "philological and onomatopoeic contiguity with 'a call' is the name of that profoundly human call and calling for worldwide solidarity with Gaza," writes Gana, is the epiphany which calls both Kanafani and Mustafa "to get over their old melancholizing habits of mind and embark on the conscious decolonial task of melancholicization by processing Nadia's selfless ethics and enlisting in the 'uprising of melancholy.'"[15]

Here Gani quotes Kanafani's text: "Everything in this [new] Gaza rose in sadness over Nadia's amputated leg from the top of the thigh. It was not the kind of sadness that stopped at weeping. It was defiance; even more than that, it was something akin to the restoration of the amputated leg!"[16] Nadia's amputated leg, her loss, which comes to symbolise the collective loss of Palestinian life and culture, becomes a literary strategy to look through the city with a different look: "he underscores its overall psych political role in spawning a collective upsurge of grievance," in a way that resonates and has

38 *Imagination Besieged*

affinities with Ahmed's idea of feminist sadness as ground for analysis and action. Gani contends

> Paradoxically, it is Nadia's amputated leg that propels forward the indefatigable pursuit of Palestinian liberation. The question is no longer about what is lost in Nadia's lost leg but rather about the range of possibilities opened up by the injustice of the loss, not least of which is the revitalization of the struggle to restore the heretofore compromised human dignity and national sovereignty.[17]

The speaker invests the void of the amputated leg as a locus of a new national consciousness. It is not only Nadia's loss but also the void created by the erasure and ethnic cleansing of Palestinians. Kanafani's protagonist refuses to run away or to give up the sadness that comes from the loss of life and culture, and in this sense, he insists on staying with this loss not to mourn it, but to retool the melancholic feeling he had experienced in leaving Gaza. This is different from Melusina's cry, which seems to lead to a form of an intimate mourning.

In his letter, Kanafani is clear: "This obscure feeling that you had as you left Gaza, this small feeling must grow into a giant deep within you. It must expand, you must seek it to find yourself, here among the ugly debris of defeat." In his words, this melancholy that grips Mustafa and those who are forced to leave to find better life conditions somewhere else must grow, as the realisation of the necessity of continuing the collective struggle for liberation.

Kanafani's words echo those of Simone Weil quoted early on, whose uncompromising position is clear when it insists that, as long as human suffering exists, individual consolation is impossible, and mourning cannot take place for injustices and violence that are ongoing. This void cannot and must not be filled with tears and attempts to move on, but it must make us uncomfortable. Against normalising violence and suffering and making it bearable, Weil reminds us that we must not get used to suffering and normalising violence; she writes, in a way that resonates with Kanafani, "May our sense of reality not be dissolved by this thought but made more intense."[18]

If the past appears tragic, the present perpetual, and the future impossible, how to speak from the space of this future impossible? How to pay attention and bear witness to the "sight unseen," the invisible losses, the un grievable ones? How to tell a story when we are at loss for words and don't have a language to articulate the loss and pain?

If, as scholar Marianne Hirsch argues, the preservation of traumatic memories is not a simple operation of a nostalgic mind but motivates the younger generations to seek justice, we might read with these melancholy acts of reinscribing loss as "upheavals of sadness."

It is this feeling that emerges by reading Adania Shibli's novel *Minor Detail*.[19] The "minor detail" that sets the novel in motion is a date: August 2,

Movement 1 39

which coincides both with the birthday of the protagonist of the novel, a young Palestinian journalist, and the disappearance and murder of a young Bedouin woman 25 years earlier. In 2003, an article published in Haaretz made public the IDF records and the events that occurred on August 12, 1949, when a patrol led by Officer Second Lieutenant Moshe encountered three unarmed Bedouin men and a woman in her teens. After reading the article, the Palestinian journalist decides to follow the traces of the Bedouin woman and her murderers and decides to embark on a potentially dangerous journey to travel from Ramallah towards the South.

Minor Details is divided into two parts. In the first, we witness the events that led to the violence: the soldiers setting up their tents, under the scorching heat of August, the ruins left by the expulsion of Palestinians in 1948 known as the Nakba, the soldiers moving through the dunes in search of weapons, and the abduction of the girl. In the second part, the protagonist of the novel starts investigating the story. She wants to tell the story from the perspective of the victim, to restore agency to what she describes as "still-moaning black mass"—a woman whose life has been taken because she has dared to resist her rapist, to protest their inhumane treatment. According to the IDF trial records, the soldiers took the girl, and once arrived back at the camp, the platoon sergeant stripped the prisoner naked and ordered that she be washed in a public outdoor shower and got her hair chopped off. Shibli observes, "a few tiny black ringlets of hair remained scattered across the sand." This minor detail is one of the many details which helps the author observes and describes how the events are inscribed in the landscape; minor details that apparently bear no specific significance but almost "steal" a moment of ambiguous beauty. The lieutenant later ordered her to be carried out unconscious, "because there is a stink coming off her," he said. The next day, after she complained of her treatment, the young woman was driven out into the desert, shot in the head, and buried in the sand.

The young woman from Ramallah embarks on a dangerous trip South, towards a site beyond the zone permitted by her ID card, but her journey is interrupted—too much contradictory information, too little access, and the reality of a truth that is that of the perpetrators, since she will never be able to listen to the testimony of the young woman or gain access to the evidences. The truth remains "owned" by the Israeli authorities. She remains, for much of the world, a "nobody" as Shibli writes: "and will forever remain a nobody whose voice nobody will hear." The re-inscription of loss poses for the writer a question of language. Of how to tell a story that is not supposed to be known and shared; a story whose only documents and witness accounts are written in the language of the colonisers. It is questioning the silence around the events of a violent murder and seeking out another language to articulate collective pain.

In the novel, the present is haunted by the past. The young woman, who embarked on such a dangerous trip to do justice to the story, cannot fulfil her longing, since the occupation puts obstacles on her way, denying her

40 *Imagination Besieged*

the possibility to give voice to the plea of the Palestinian people and their grievances. The catastrophic events and the violence of the occupation are not a metaphor, nor do they belong to history, but are still ongoing. Her attempt to retrace the story of the Bedioun's woman murder brings her closer to the impossibility of reconstituting it. While she is unable to mourn as she cannot solve the circumstances of the murder, the journey itself becomes a testament to the many ways in which Palestinians are deprived of their right to history.

The absence of her testimony relegates the story of the young Bedouin woman not to the past, but to a present that doesn't seem to cease to exist: a present characterised by an atmosphere of violence that can be breathed, felt, touched, and observed in the minor details of the story. The moment of defeat sharpens the protagonist's sense of ethical responsibility. There is neither a happy ending nor a brighter future to move on and beyond. It is at this point that the protagonist of the story lets go of the idea of recovering and redressing.

If sadness is the condition of critical thinking, then the protagonists of Alvaro, Kanafani, and Shibli's story all share their sadness for a loss that also manifests as a question of language. Of the kind of language that would be needed to "unearth" these buried stories; of the new language necessary to articulate a form of refusal and resistance to the occupation; of the kind of language that" listens to," as an ethical and poetic predisposition. And yet, it is precisely this loss of words that, paradoxically, becomes the impetus towards articulating grief as grievances. Alvaro writes about the misery and harsh living and working conditions in which Calabrians had been forced to live for centuries, trying to speak from the perspective of a Calabrian; Nadia's sacrifice and her loss offer a new language to the poet to speak about return as a form of resistance. Shibli's novel is one in which the protagonist seeks out a language to articulate her own viewpoint as Palestinian. It is a sense of responsibility that, in all cases, moves the story and the storytelling—feeling the losses rather than escaping them and turning the impossibility of expressing grief into the articulation of grievances and the imagination of different futures.

Notes

1 Sarah Ahmed, "Dated Feminists," blog post, 2014. Available through: https://feministkilljoys.com/2014/04/08/dated-feminists/
2 Rob Nixon writes of slow violence: "a violence that occurs gradually and out of sight." p. 15.
3 Simone Weil, *Gravity and Grace*, translated by Emma Crawford and Mario von der Ruhr (London: Routledge, 2002), p. 14.
4 Sigmund Freud, "Mourning and Melancholia," *Standard Edition of the Complete Psychological Works of Sigmund Freud*, vol. 14 (1914–1916), edited and translated by James Strachey et al. (London: Hogarth Press), 243–258.

Movement I 41

5 Hélène Cixous, "Coming to Writing" and Other Essays. With an Introductory Essay by Susan Rubin Suleiman. Edited by Deborah Jenson. Translated by Sarah Cornell.

6 Hélène Cixous, *Readings. The Poetics of Blanchot, Joyce, Kafka, Kleist, Lispector, and Tsvetayeva* (University Minnesota Press, 1991).

7 Corrado Alvaro, "Il Ritratto di Melusina," in *L'Amata alla finestra*, collana I grandi tascabili, introduzione di Walter Pedullà, bibliografia di Massimo Onofri, cronologia di Pietro De Marchi, n. 347, Milano, Bompiani, 1994. All translations are mine.

8 Ibid.

9 Ibid.

10 Ibid.

11 Gana, Nouri, *Melancholy Acts: Defeat and Cultural Critique in the Arab World* (New York, NY, 2023; online edn, Fordham Scholarship Online, 18 Jan. 2024), Introduction, p. 19.

12 Ibid, p. 21.

13 Ibid, p. 24.

14 Ibid, p. 25.

15 Ibid, p. 25.

16 Ibid, p. 25.

17 Ibid, p. 26.

18 Simone Weil, *Gravity and Grace*, translated by Emma Crawford and Mario von der Ruhr (London: Routledge, 2002), p. 14.

19 Adania Shibli, *Minor Detail* (Fitzcarraldo Editions, 2020).

4 Movement II: Even When They Are Dangerous, Examine the Heart of Those Machines You Hate[1]

The histories of feminism are full of examples of women who rebelled to their faith to express their different viewpoints on the world. They have been portrayed as terrible for having challenged hierarchies of power and systems of oppression. Their anger is not vengeful, as it has been portrayed, but rather it involves, as Sara Ahmed argues, "a reading of the world in a particular way, and also involves a reading of the reading; so, identifying as a feminist is dependent upon taking that anger as the grounds for a critique of the world."[2] Feminist anger is a question of language, of seeking out a language to observe and gain insights into the materialities of oppression.

Feminist anger is both a symptom and a response in the form of a refusal to "move beyond the histories of injuries" and to become innocent subject and perfect victim. It is not a mythical revenge over the male world (as the patriarchal world would like us to believe), but the energy to react against deep social and psychic investments in racism as well as sexism. Feminist anger thus, as Ahmed argues following Audre Lorde, can become a source and a tool of insights into the multiple ways in which violence and aggression manifest: "If anger is a form of 'againstness,' then it is precisely about the impossibility of moving beyond the history of injuries to a pure or innocent position."[3]

Indeed, in making use of anger, one decides to stand in a position of protest. But this antagonism doesn't have to become a wall and the impossibility of communication. It might manifest in creative terms as the necessity to find a language to articulate common grievances and keep privileges in check. Against the dismissal of "anger" as unproductive and negative, Lorde poses anger as a problem of language and insists on a "use" of anger that is self-reflective, patient, and insightful.

Anger, Lorde observes, must be listened to, contextualise, reflected upon, reckoned with, and most of all used creatively as a source of insights and actions, because it often discloses something deeper, linked to the experience of structural violence that triggers it.[4] Lorde invites other feminists to reckon with the oppressor and the oppressive behaviours, micro-aggression, and internalised violence by paying attention to the "uses" of language and the violence it carries in the world.

DOI: 10.4324/9781003492634-5

Movement II 43

Anger is too often and conveniently addressed as unjustified response—a little too much, inappropriate and unacceptable. I've myself been addressed as an angry woman, and while my anger was presented to me as disproportionate, unexpected, a "passionate" temperament, and, at times, a problem to be fixed, I insisted on to remain angry in the face of what I perceived as abuse, aggression, manipulation, or violation, a way of signalling a boundary has been crossed. People are often uncomfortable with the expression of anger, and for good reason, as it can be extremely destructive. However, there are moments in which anger might come as a response to oppressive behaviours. If "anger" makes people so uncomfortable, what could possibly cause discomfort?

In this essay, I wish to address anger as a historically defined affect, and alongside Lorde, as a question of finding a language to express what is often difficult to express in the language we have at our disposal—a language that, as Lorde argues, is meant to divide, erase, separate, and violate. I look here at manifestations of anger as a social response to oppressive conditions in the specific context of Calabria. What the stories have in common is the ways in which anger becomes a "luxury" for those seeking freedom. And yet, it also pays attention to the ways in which their protagonists have found ways to articulate anger in the forms of protest and resistance.

Greek mythology is full of angry gods. In his "Hymn to Demeter," Homer describes the goddess Demeter's anger at the rape and kidnapping of her daughter in the following words:

> In her anger at the one who is known for his dark clouds, the son of Kronos, she shunned the company of gods and lofty Olympus. She went away, visiting the cities of humans, with all their fertile landholdings, shading over her appearance, for a long time. And not one of men, looking at her, could recognize her. Not one of women, either, who are accustomed to wear their girdles low-slung.[5]

Violence and loss are the foundational moments of this tale. Demeter wandered the planet aimlessly in search of her child. And she is "lost" in her grief [*akhos*]. The violent kidnapping and rape of her daughter, Persephone, by the underworld god Hade, is the "sad event" that sets Demeter on her painful journey. Anger here translates into a series of catastrophes. First, she protests by refusing the company of the gods in the Olympus, and then, by casting a long shadow on the fertile land, she refuses to bear the fruit of the earth.

Her self is scattered and dispersed, but in fact, she is not lost. Her pain and suffering, as we are told by Homer, make her unrecognisable to others—not one man, not one among the women, can recognise her. She is monstrous, and in her monstrosity, she becomes fury that undoes what it touches: she rips open the arid soil and causes famine, diseases, and death. Zeus and Hades, responsible for the violence and its reparation, become undone too.

44 *Imagination Besieged*

Anger threatens the hierarchy of gods. The goddess refuses to accept her unfortunate fate. However, this anger is not simply and only destructive of an existing order. Anger doesn't have to become destructive. It is also the energy that transforms Demeter's grief into the expression of a grievance, and she travels and brings her protest into the world; a grievance forming a community of protest around the violent act; people taking part in this "upheaval of sadness." Anger tears Demeter apart, but at the same time, it enables the goddess to articulate her demand very clearly, that her daughter be brought back from the underworld. And the goddess's articulation of her grief into a generative anger also propels the creation of the Eleusinian mysteries, the festivities dedicated to the goddess and celebrated in ancient times everywhere in Greece and *Magnia Grecia*.

The rituals linked to the festivities were an important moment for the whole community. The loss of familial love that Demeter experiences is reenacted by the initiation of the cult, also known as the Mysteries, in a festival known as the Thesmophoria. Women initiated to the cult were acting out the rape of Persephone, sacrificial and orgiastic rituals were performed in celebration of the mourning and healing of the goddess' grief.

Clement of Alexandria writes that part of the rituals consisted of making offering to the goddess by slaughtering and throwing piglets as well as vegetables and fruit such as pomegranate into pits called "megara." The rotten remains would later be collected and brought to the altar, "they believe that anyone who takes some and sows it with their seed will have a good crop."[6] The Mysteries draws a new cartography of the relationship between spiritual and material, between life and death, love and loss, between grief and joy.

In her interpretation of the myth, Italian feminist philosopher Adriana Cavarero reads Demeter as the figure of an original matricide and the expression of a different relation to life and death, mother and daughter. Through a retrieval of the mother's gaze, Cavarero establishes a reading of these relationships that embodied, and not abstract, a certain way of seeing.[7] This way of seeing is defined by a disinvestment from the order of death and the claim to the life-giving power of the feminine, in turning anger into a possibility of articulating a different worldview, a new language of liberation, and that liberates itself from the need of reproducing patriarchal and colonial violence.

In the Homeric work, there are at least fourteen words for anger, some are *ólunthos, phélēks, sûkon, iskhás, orgḗ, thumós, khólos, kótos*, and *mênis*. If anger translates an intense experience of pain into the possibility of transformation and life, in the specific context of my region, Calabria, and its histories of violence, I wonder how can this anger bring insights and give birth to a new language of liberation? I treat anger here as symptoms of the living legacy of the histories of violence in the present.

Anger is not only an expression of personal attitudes but also historically grounded. Aggressiveness is considered almost a natural trait of many Mediterranean cultures. However, it is necessary to recall that this stereotypical

Movement II 45

image of the southern as naturally aggressive was built over time by a colonial mentality which in the nineteenth century was spreading with the Imperial expansion and through the disciplines, among others, of ethnography, anthropology, and archaeology. The construction of aggressiveness and passivity as a dominant psychic affective complex in Calabrian society must be considered in its historical and social context, as anthropologists such as Vito Teti have done. It must be considered in relation to occupations, revolts, the phenomenon of brigands, and the exploitative conditions in which the population lived.

Anger did not assume the transformative power of decolonisation. Rather, all attempts have been made to repressed, suffocated, and often dismissed it as irrational, criminal; an isolated disruptive events, and the expression of a bilious and melancholic people. This naturalisation of the "violent character" and of anger as pathological often served the colonial discourse in justifying oppression and in domesticating the "other." Cesare Lombroso, in his *In Calabria* (1862), identifies in the bilious temperament—together with a "proud soul, irascible, stubborn, fearless, eager to dominate, to the point of arrogance, lover of fighting, of pleasures, but full of intelligence"[8]—the constitutive trait of the personality of the Calabrian people. Vito Teti notes, "Black bile, to which he traces numerous diseases (hepatitis, gallstones and visceral obstructions), is inserted in an organicist conception."[9] Both angry and melancholic, the "Mediterranean type" belongs to the cursed race—idleness, apathy, degeneration, tiredness, inertia, dirt, violence, and superstition were considered among the causes of the "backwardness of the south."[10]

In *Maledetto Sud*, Vito Teti observes that Calabria was constructed and perceived as a place of extreme and radical distance and that the many foreign travellers, who, in the golden age of the Grand Tour, ventured through the "extreme" provinces, were placed on guard against going to the "cursed lands": Described by the Jesuits as the "Indias de por acà" (The Indias of Here), where the inhabitants appeared "all from the forest," as in 1561 Giovanni Xavier wrote; or Calabria "Africa," according to an eighteenth–nineteenth-century image, in all these accounts, Calabria was represented an exotic and difficult place. Before even they were able to talk about themselves, Calabrians were described by foreigners as "barbarian, primitive, degenerate, senile, degraded, cursed, filthy, idle, brigand, nostalgic, violent, excessive, ambiguous, criminal, superstitious."[11]

But, why were Calabrians so degraded and barbarians? In 1960, the Calabrian historian Umberto Caldora published an interesting investigative volume entitled *Calabria Napoleonica*, which analyses the lives of Calabrians during the two decades of French rule. In his preface, he observes that at the time Calabrians were "demoralized, deluded, sceptical and exasperated, and especially analphabet. The devastating earthquake of 1783 had inflicted a hard blow to the inhabitants."[12] Caldora observes that the period between 1800 and 1806 is perhaps one of the saddest of the Kingdom. On the one hand, the local population had facilitated the French invasion; having experienced a

46 *Imagination Besieged*

worsening of the repression and their life conditions, however, many, eventually, joined groups of brigands and became involved in a series of revolts that mark the modern history of this region.

Everyone was trying to take advantage of the general chaos in a situation dominated by "the hunger of land." The Italian unity did not ease the conditions of the Calabrian population. In the more than 100 years since the "integration" of the south into the vision of national unit, the struggle for the land and against oppressive conditions remained deeply unchanged. By the late 1940s, peasants had occupied the land. How could the Calabrian peasants not be angry after centuries of oppressive economic and social conditions and so many false promises?

The peasant revolts culminated in the deaths of several peasants in Melissa in 1949, when farmworkers occupying the land clashed with the local landowners, and their men and the police. The Carabinieri opened fire, and two people were killed, as well as many injured and arrested.

Among those killed was Angelina Romeo, whose forgotten story, is told by Maria Concetta Preta in the short-story, *Riprendersi la terra. Angelina Mauro e la strage di Melissa*[13](To take back the land. Angela Maura and the massacre of Melissa). Angelina is described by Preta in the following words,

> she was a peasant. She was not doing politics, poor thing, like all the other women from a humble background, she had a vague idea of the Italian nation. Killed by bullets that hit her in the kidney, she had reached the Fragalà estate on a donkey. A female voice, funeral lament from a greek chorus, she cries after seeing her collapsing to the ground, 'Mammazì, l'avimu patuta.'

> And then concludes, "Today noone brings flowers to Angelina's grave, no one knows of the little bee from Melissa."[14]

The desire underlining Preta's short story is to keep telling the stories of those women who have been erased from official history books, but whose experience might be an example of resistance and an inspiration for the younger generations in the fight against social injustices. Preta's short story has a pedagogical value in a region and a country in which the shadow of 'ndrangheta looms heavily in everyone's everyday life. It teaches that Calabrians, and especially Calabrian women, are not, or not only, as they have been described, remissive and enslaved to the patriarchal or the 'ndrangheta logic. They are autonomous, fierce, and rebellious, and they have contributed enormously to the well-being and sustenance of their communities. But they have also paid for their uncompromising refusal with their lives.

The fertile land kissed by the sun is where the 'ndrangheta[15] plants the seeds of illegality and imposes its own rules with threads and intimidations. Author John Dickie has observed in his history of mafia[16] that through political

Movement II 47

corruption, extortion rackets, and cocaine trafficking, although coming from the poorest region, 'ndrangheta' is the most feared and richest criminal organisation. They control ports and agricultural production, forcing field workers to be exploited and work for few euros per day, as well as facilitate and make benefits out of human tragedies through human trafficking and extortion of refugees who arrive in Calabria to work picking olives, oranges, and tomatoes in often inhumane and undignified conditions.

In January 2010, a group of African migrant workers took to the streets of Rosarno, in the province of Reggio Calabria, to protest and denounce the dehumanising working and living conditions in which farm workers are forced to live, in abandoned factories with no electricity, current water, and with shelters made of cardboard boxes. The riots were triggered by the attack by two Italian youths who opened fire from a car and wounded two workers who were earning their money picking fruit. The intimidations did not start the day of the aggression. Other times African workers had already protested in peaceful manners. This time it was different. They set fire to rubbish bins, destroying shop windows and damaged cars, engaging in a sort of street battle with the police.

The anger was triggered not by the singular event, as many wanted to believe, but by years and years of institutional neglect, social exclusion, exploitation, and continuous dehumanisation. It was the same anger that more than 50 years earlier had brought Angelina to join the occupation of the land and got her killed. These times, to be exploited were not Calabrians, but poorly paid African migrants. Although the exploitative and violent conditions have remained unchanged, even for Calabrians living in the region, it was difficult for many to see the "longue durée" of these forms of exploitation and recognise in the act of anger a last desperate attempt for the migrant workers to make their voices heard.

Sarah Ahmed has observed how difficult it is when anger is expressed by a black or brown person in a social context in which, "reasonable, thoughtful arguments are dismissed as anger (which of course empties anger of its own reason), which makes you angry, such that your response becomes read as the confirmation of evidence that you are not only angry but also unreasonable!"[17] The anger of the African land workers was quickly dismissed as irrational, savage, unreasonable; the immigrants relocated, and the shanty town they had built and lived in were destroyed. The exposure of violence always risks becoming the origin of violence. At that moment, the Calabrian community of Rosarno failed to see in the migrants' anger the expression of their own frustration with the feeling of being abandoned by a state which has repeatedly failed to give answers and offer practical solutions to what were conveniently described as "crisis," but in fact were problems that could have been solved.

As it has been with the peasant revolts in the mid-1940s, so the protest was quickly dismissed as "violent" and the former interior minister Roberto Maroni, from the xenophobic Lega Nord, called this the result of "too much

48 *Imagination Besieged*

tolerance towards clandestine immigration."[18] Not surprisingly, the state put the blame on the victims of the attacks, rather than addressing the illegal exploitation of labour and the breach of basic human rights which had triggered the migrants' anger. Instead, the migrants had to carry the burden of the violence, and their anger was perceived as a sign of an "uncivilised" people. The response was police repression and the eventual relocation of some migrants.

The revolts were unprecedented[19] in the more recent history of the region. It was, as the former head of Italy's parliamentary anti-mafia commission observed, "the first time the African immigrants rebel against the local 'ndrangheta which dominates the fruit and vegetable business...during the protests they even surrounded the house of an old boss in the Pesce clan, which is a powerful local family, something Calabrians have never done."[20] Could, something that, in the eyes of the locals and national authorities, seem as naïve as the anger and courage to confront the local 'ndrangheta boss, be the beginning of a different path and a different story to be told?

In September 2019, a United Nations report denounced the conditions of farm workers in Southern Italy, which, as it is written, amount to contemporary forms of slavery. The report noted that "'workers' rights are often violated and they may be exposed to severe exploitation or slavery."[21] The story of African migrant workers in Southern Italy is deeply connected to the histories of violence and the technologies of governmentality that today, have made the Mediterranean a dangerous militarised border.

In the present, anger is often, as the events of Rosarno show, a luxury not afforded to everyone equally. The migrants risk deportation, and the local politicians exploit their electorates' anger for their personal gains. The events of Rosarno did not change the community's perception of the migrants. The resonance that the events had, however, raised the level of awareness and brought the problem once again to the public attention. But this has not resulted necessary in a language to articulate for migrants and locals, a common grievance, and thus a possibility of solidarity. Very often the language used by media to describe migrants is paternalistic and racist.

What have failed revolts and unfulfilled promises to do with anger? Because they are stories of resistance against injustices which contradict the well-rehearsed narrative that these are just "episodes of violence" and as such should be ignored. Whether in the revolt of the Calabrian peasants or in the African workers revolt of Rosarno, anger too often gets quickly instrumentalised by mass media and institutions to condemn as "irrational" the migrants' anger and legitimise police's use of force. But rarely migrants themselves are given voice. Too often portrayed as victims of this or that violence, they remain locked in the position of the "other."

For this anger to become insightful, it would require a new critical way of seeing that acknowledges the grievances of the other rather than dismissing them; engaging in a dialogue that seeks to clarify, rather than obfuscate,

Movement II 49

the discomfort. It would demand, as Egyptian activist Alaa Abd El-Fattah writes, that we mobilise the moments of anger and those of joy in "inventing a new discourse of resistance free of the vocabulary monopolized by the factions."[22]

Notes

1 Audre Lorde, "For Each Of You." Available through: https://www.poetrynook.com/poem/each-you
2 Sara Ahmed, "Feminist Attachment", in *The Cultural Politics of Emotion* (Edinburgh: Edinburgh University Press, 2014), 168–190.
3 Sara Ahmed, "it's not the time for a party," blog, 2015. Available through: https://feministkilljoys.com/2015/05/13/it-is-not-the-time-for-a-party/
4 Audre Lorde, "The Uses of Anger. Women Respond to Racism," in Sister Outsider: Essays and Speeches. "Women of Color in America have grown up within a symphony of anger at being silenced at being unchosen, at knowing that when we survive, it is in spite of a world that takes for granted our lack of humanness, and which hates our very existence outside of its service. And I say "symphony" rather than "cacophony" because we have had to learn to orchestrate those furies so that they do not tear us apart. We have had to learn to move through them and use them for strength and force and insight within our daily lives."
5 Available through: https://uh.edu/~cldue/texts/demeter.html#_ftn5
6 Giulia Sfameni Gasparro, "Aspects of the Cult of Demetra in Magna Grecia," in Casadio G., Johnston P.A., Mystic Cults in Magnia Grecia (University of Texas Press, 2009).
7 Adriana Cavarero, *In Spite of Plato*. Polity Press, 1995 "birth calls for a dual system of the gaze: one between the mother and the daughter, the other between the mother and the son. It is because in the myth of origin the son decides to distract himself and turn his attention to death, exiling the daughter there, that the gaze between the mother and the daughter is forcibly interrupted. Therefore, after this act, in the patriarchal symbolic order, neither the son nor the daughter look at the mother, the physis. But while the son can decide to do so, the daughter has been violently prevented from looking," p. 27.
8 Cesare Lombroso, *In Calabria* (1892), Rubettino.
9 Vito Teti, *Maledetto Sud*, Einaudi, 2015.
10 Ibid.
11 Ibid.
12 F. Mastroberti, La Calabria nel Decennio Francese, p. 148.
13 Maria Concetta Preta, *Riprendersi la terra. Angelina Mauro e la strage di Melissa (1949)*.
With these words, Preta describes the night before the tragic events: "Walking in the dark along the clay mule track, the women advance without a complaint: Onna Cuncia and Grazia Palà, with children on their laps, Maria Ferraro, Angelina Mauro, and many others, with baskets of food and barrels of water balanced on their heads. They arrive on the land at dawn and take up spades, hoes, and rakes to remove the shrubs and air the soil. At midday, the women uncover the lunch they brought from home and eat it with canes carved like forks. When work resumes, the Celere appears, people greet, soon silenced by the sound of the shots, by the bodies: Francesco Nigro and Giovanni Zito fall first, Angelina Mauro falls, hit in the kidney while raising her flag towards the sun." Available through: https://www.comune.noale.ve.it/materiale-pari-opportunita/

50 *Imagination Besieged*

14 Maria Concetta Preta, *Riprendersi la terra. Angelina Mauro e la strage di Melissa.* Available through: https://www.comune.noale.ve.it/materiale-pari-opportunita/

15 The 'ndranghetista are notorious for their brutality and cruelty and their blind devotion to their leaders. In the '90s and early '00s, the central authorities turned a blind eye to their activities, and the local authorities didn't hesitate to collaborate with them and have often granted their leaders immunity from prosecution. And while many films and literary works have romanticised the figure of the "mafioso" (Il Padrino is a well-known example, but also Gomorra, or the Soprano, just to mention a few), making it into an international recognised southern Italian type, the truth is, as Alberto Saviano among others have represented in his literary works, that 'Ndrangheta is fundamentally hostile towards society, and their anti-social tendencies might well be considered a kind of distorted version of anti-authoritarian attitudes typical of marginalised groups, but the truth is, they are responsible for the "backwardness" and the brutality of our society; they are an obstacle to any positive change, and they're co-responsible for the continuous state of "emergency" and the permanent crisis Calabria live through on a daily basis.

16 John Dickie, *Cosa Nostra: A History of the Sicilian Mafia*, St. Martin's Griffin; First Edition (October 21, 2005).

17 Sara Ahmed, "Feminist Killjoys (And Other Willful Subjects)," in *Poliphonic Feminisms. Acting in Concert.* Available through: http://sfonline.barnard.edu/polyphonic/ahmed_04.htm (last accessed September 2021).

18 See Domenico Perrotta, 7 Gennaio 2010: La Rivolta di Rosarno, Il Mulino, blog, 2020. Available through: https://www.rivistailmulino.it/a/7-gennaio-2010; CGIL – FILCAM, Immigrati, una giornata di guerriglie a Rosarno. Available through: https://www.filcams.cgil.it/article/rassegna_stampa/immigrati_una_giornata_di_guerriglia_a_rosarno; Veronica Iesué, "Rosarno: Una ribellione ancora oggi inascoltata," in *Cronache di Ordinario Razzismo*, online, 2020. Available through: https://www.cronachediordinariorazzismo.org/libro-bianco/rosarno-una-ribellione-ancora-oggi-inascoltata/; Alessia Candito, "Viaggio a Rosarno sette anni dopo la rivolta," in La Repubblica.it, 2017. Available through: https://www.repubblica.it/solidarieta/immigrazione/2017/01/10/news/rosarno_neve_migranti-155720756/

19 Domenico Perrotta observes, the revolts of Rosarno had at least three important effects: increased the awareness of the Italian and European public opinion regarding the working conditions of the people who pick the food we found in our supermarket; it became unavoidable to address the question of shelter and decent living conditions for the workers; secondly, since the facts of Rosarno and a year later, in August 2011, a strike called by African workers in another rural centre in the South, Nardò, in Salento, pushed individuals and organisations to engage in support of migrant agricultural workers, sometimes together with them. Associations, trade unions, NGOs, religious organisations, and critical consumer groups: the social, economic, trade union, and political intervention projects of these ten years are countless. Third, the event prompted local institutions and national governments to take action on the issue. Two national laws (August 2011 and November 2016) introduce and modify article 603 bis of the Criminal Code, redefining the rules on combating gang mastering and labour exploitation.

20 Tom Kington, Italians cheer as police move African immigrants out after clashes with locals in *The Guardian* online, 2010. Available through: https://www.theguardian.com/world/2010/jan/10/calabria-mafia-africa-immigration

21 International Labour Organization, "Forced Labour, modern slavery and trafficking in persons" report. Available through: https://www.ilo.org/topics/forced-labour-modern-slavery-and-trafficking-persons

22 Alaa Abd El-Fattah, *You Have Not Yet Been Defeated* (Seven Stories Press, 2021).

5 Colourless Knickknacks (After Fanon)

All the Mediterranean values—the triumph of the human individual, of clarity, and of beauty—become lifeless, colorless knickknacks. All those speeches seem like collections of dead words; those values which seemed to uplift the soul are revealed as worthless, simply because they have nothing to do with the concrete conflict in which the people is engaged.[1]

In his address *Indigenous Culture: The New Mediterranean Culture*,[2] delivered at the *Masoin de la Culture* in Algier in 1937, Camus insisted on the recognition of a new Mediterranean culture born from the desire to rally against and contrast Fascism and Nazism's appropriation of Roman's history to legitimise their claims to cultural and moral superiority. The speech has at its central argument the consolidation of a "Mediterranean community" that would express the cultural connections between indigenous people and European settlers living in colonial Algeria.

Camus discredited other visions of the Mediterranean and made a claim that the "east" is the "true" Mediterranean culture against the Latin West. Yet, like many European intellectuals before and after him, he continued to refer to mostly the limited Greek lineage, effectively excluding the Arab and Islamic cultures from this idea of belonging. The disregard for these contributions to the formation of Western identity and history has been a trend in western research and academic studies for a long time. The foundational texts of classical Mediterranean anthropology, as historian and anthropologist Joseph Viscomi argues, "have paid little attention to the real connections and separations that constitute Mediterranean places,"[3] often taking the "Mediterranean" for granted, on the premise that the Mediterranean itself is already there. Literary scholar Roberto Dainotto also notes that "Any Italian could write about the Mediterranean... without bothering to mention Abdelkebir Khatibi, Albert Memmi or Taieb Belghazi. For a Turkish or Algerian author, however, it is impossible (or suicidal) not to deal with the 'Mediterranean' canonized in European literature."[4]

DOI: 10.4324/9781003492634-6

52 *Imagination Besieged*

In this sense, the "Mediterranean" culture (where the term "Mediterranean" is bracketed to mark its problematic histories) as a cultural and political project was destined to remain a European fantasy that pretends to unite into a single political and cultural project all the interests of the regions into a single (European) area of influence. Fanon, however, as the passage quoted at the beginning of the essay states, rejects this fantasy of unity and reminds the reader that this vision of a "Mediterranean community" couldn't move the natives, who were too aware of the European "civilisation" missions.

In the process of decolonisation, Fanon argues, the colonised refuses both the values and words of the French intellectual colonialists, who pathologised any form of resistance, as well as the opinions of progressive intellectuals, who promoted a peaceful, non-violent neutral affirmation of the "rights" of all people to "freedom" and "justice" under the banner of Western humanism.

Unmasked in all its violence and its hypocrisy, the culture of the coloniser makes words such as "human individual, clarity, and beaty," sound like "lifeless," Fanon writes, a collection of "dead-words" and "colorless knick-knacks." Every time these values are mentioned, he observes, "they produce in the native a sort of stiffening or muscular lockjaw."[5] This muscular tension finds release either as internal self-implosive auto-destructive violence or, Fanon insists, as a force of decolonisation.

In this sense, the language of the coloniser results in insufficient, problematic, stiffening, and suffocating of the aspiration and desire for freedom of the Algerians. The hostility towards the "Mediterranean" is thus the refusal to accept, as Fanon writes, "the violence with which the supremacy of white values is affirmed and the aggressiveness which has permeated the victory of these values over the ways of life and of thought of the native."[6] Another language becomes necessary thus: one that refuses the coloniser's cultural supremacy, perpetuating racial violence while promoting whiteness as measure of civilisation.

In *Orientalism* (1978), Said highlighted the rhetorical use that of this term has been made for what he calls "illegitimate political ends"—that is, the instrumental and ideological use that determined the affirmation of the idea of the Mediterranean as an undifferentiated unity, defined by backwardness as an excuse for policies that have profited the Northern regions and which determine their contested cultural and economic "superiority."[7] The "Mediterranean" is not only a contested idea, but it can also be conceived, as a point of departure for a critique of the politics this concept implies; it must become the location of a questioning of national identities, narratives and forms of representation that have reproduced erasure, destining this region to live in the past, and hindering the imagination of different Mediterranean futures.

At the same time, can the "Mediterranean" become the locus for imagining new alliances? For this task, a new language must emerge capable of carrying the contradictions, the paradoxes, the different visions and viewpoints, and the multifaceted realities of this region. The "Mediterranean" is not a geography,

Colourless Knickknacks (After Fanon) 53

an idea, or an identity to be given for granted. Instead, it has proven time and again to be an elusive and contested location.

Both scholars and historians disagree about almost everything that matters: its physical boundaries, its primary characteristics, its unity, its connectivity, and the value of its past and future as a space for political projects, economic ties, cultural connections, and meaningful opportunities.[8] Fanon's critical take on this fantasy of a Mediterranean unity becomes relevant when today we witness a sort of uncritical and ahistorical exaltation, a romanticisation of what constitutes the "Mediterranean," that often hides commercial interests and political agendas.[9]

Ian Chambers and Tiziana Terranova aptly describe the Mediterranean as a "colonial lake,"[10] an idyllic vacation destination where tourists contemplate the origins of Western civilisation as "reified in its archaeological ruins," swim in the turquoise sea, and enjoy the benefits of the Mediterranean diet: "Tourists can fly on a cheap easyjet flight to Tel Aviv to attend the love parade and enjoy the beautiful beaches, while ignoring the ongoing occupation."[11] The Mediterranean is thus described as both a tourist destination and the laboratory for "the development and testing of new technologies for the government of mobility, the securing of borders, and military policing."[12] To this, I would add the psychodynamic effects of those histories and present policies.

The colonial matrix that organises the Mediterranean at the intersection of Europe, Africa, and Asia tries to obfuscate the possibility of grasping these intersections, sedimentations, movements, the differences, paradoxes, and contradictions that characterise this geopolitical space. "The common cultural heritage," Isabelle Schäfer observes, "has continued to be invoked while firm policies on security, migration and enlargement are pursued, which draw a clear frontier at the centre of the Mediterranean."[13] The Mediterranean is thus a paradox. European Union politics, on the one hand, promotes a shared Euro-Mediterranean identity, and on the other hand, it constructs the South and East as "dependent antechambers of Europe."

Immigration, economic crisis, and war have all drawn attention to the Mediterranean as an area of instability, in need of guidance and reform, promoting economic and cultural alliances that in fact obfuscate the pursuit of European interests in the region, exactly as it has been attempted for the past 100 years. Patterns of colonialism and its global matrix are repeated; life and work are organised around the racial grammar of difference,[14] which distinguishes between "refugee," "sans-papier," and "citizen"; that defines the Jewish-Christian world as "democratic liberal" against the authoritarian illiberal "Islamic East"; that distinguishes between the technologically and economically "advanced" West and the backwards and "lacking" South and East.

The Mediterranean remains a question of the unequal distribution of power, resources, infrastructures, knowledge, and responsibilities. Thus, to think with the "Mediterranean" as a space of critical questioning means recording the limits, of our apparatus of knowledge, and engaging and drawing

54 *Imagination Besieged*

from multiple archives and a multitude of historical and cultural conditions. Or, as anthropologists Chamber and Cariello write in *The Mediterranean Question,*[15]

> Listening to the languages used to describe the Mediterranean, and crossing the spaces in which these languages are transmitted and translated, means folding and crumpling the structure of meaning received (without erasing it), thus creating a historical and critical depth that proposes a different Mediterranean, one yet to come.[16]

The language of "listening," rather than the imperative of speaking, becomes the modality of inquiry into the stories and histories buried in the depth of the Mediterranean archive. Understanding how the past influences the present means thus listening to the plurality of voices and things that emerge from this depth; accommodating different visions and ways of seeing, different spatial coordinates, cosmologies, and cosmotechnologies. To narrate the Mediterranean is a matter of responsibility towards language and memory; of questioning assimilated images of the Mediterranean, returning things to the depth of their cultural lineage and the resonance of their historical memories, in archival connection with their possible future.

Chambers and Cariello suggestively propose paying attention to the "viewpoint of the diver." Inspired by an ancient fresco found near Paestum, Campania, inside the lid of a sarcophagus and destined for invisibility, the diver of the fresco appears, as they observed: "A clearly dark body of skin that challenges the European version of Jesus Christ, the Virgin Mary and the Greek heroes who are all white and Aryan; a body that twenty-five hundred years ago descended gracefully through the air, staring wide-eyed at the future."[17] Looking through the eyes of the diver means to record those stories and things that have been neglected by history, or even worse rendered invisible, erased from memory, swallowed up by the depth of the sea.

The diver invites the observer to see and read the Mediterranean not only in the whitened marble of the Ancient Greek Acropolis but also and more importantly in the coloured skin of port cities of the ancient trade routes, in the faces of the women of Costantinopole or Palmyra, of the fishermen of Mazzara del Vallo and Tunis, in the diver of Paestum, in the sandy colours and byzantine icons of the now destroyed Orthodox Christian churches of the Gaza Strip, the merchant coming from Timbuktu, in the full spectrum of colours and influences that make this a space at the same time a border and its place of contestation.

It is the Mediterranean seen through the eyes of Marie Rose, a Christian Syrian-Lebanese woman who, during the civil war, was murdered for her "betrayal" of her ethnic belonging. Marie Rose is the protagonist of the novel by Lebanese American poet and painter Etel Adnan, *Sitt Marie Rose*, published in Paris in 1977.[18] The book is based on a real event: the capture, torture,

Colourless Knickknacks (After Fanon)   55

and death by dismemberment of a woman who had left her native community to work for Palestinian refugees. The protagonist lives in a Palestinian refugee camp in the West of Beirut with her three children and her Palestinian lover. An activist for Palestinian refugees, she directs a school for the deaf-mute in her former Christian quarter in the East. In spite of the war that broke out on April 13, 1975, she continued to go back and forth between the two halves of the divided city and the two communities. However, she is kidnapped in her former neighbourhood during a ceasefire and is killed in haste immediately after the end of the truce.

Written as a series of first-person accounts, the novel addresses a woman's resistance to what Adnan identifies as the "tribal mentality" at the heart of the Lebanese society: "[t]he allegiance of an individual to his or her family, village, tribe or clan." The civil war was both an internal Lebanese affair and a regional conflict involving also international actors. It revolved around issues including the Palestine-Israel conflict, the Cold War, Arab nationalism, and political Islam, as well as internal disagreement among the Lebanese political elites on strategic alliances.

During 15 years of fighting, more than 100,000 people lost their lives[19] and close to a million people, or two-thirds of the Lebanese population, experienced displacement. Adnan recounts the violence as seen through the eye of the protagonist, and in contrast to the male culture in the context of Lebanese Christian masculinity, "Violence rises from every square meter as if from a metallic forest (...) Kidnappings of passers-by and torture become daily events. Women stay at home more than ever. They consider war like an evening of scores between men"[20] and "Via war and violence, they think to earn authority, order, power."[21]

If for the male characters violence accelerates the progress of a people,[22] Marie Rose sees war and violence as the product of fear and terror: "It's fear, not love, that generates all actions here. The dog in the street looks at you with terror in his eyes. The combatant has the mentality of a cave man [...]"[23] This atmosphere of fear finds its expression in explosions of violence, in exaggerated and toxic expression of masculinity or religious affiliation and sectarianism. Again, Adnan writes,

> The citizens of this country are accustomed to fear, the immense fear of not deserving their mother's love, of not being first at school or in the car race, of not making love as often as the other guys at the office, of not killing as many birds as their neighbor, of being less rich than the Kuwaitis, of being less established in their history than the Syrians, of not dancing as well as the Latin-Americans, of being less of a break-neck and extremist than the Palestinian terrorists.[24]

This fear, this crisis of identity, Adnan insists, is the product of historical violence. This is rendered legible in the memories of Marie Rose and

56 *Imagination Besieged*

Mounir, a dear friend, who, as she recalls, as teenager used to dressed up like a Crusader in a white tunic while at the same time wearing an Arab "kefyeh-and-agal for a ceremony." At first, Mounir does not seem to perceive the contradiction until Marie told him, "You come from here. You are not a foreigner. You don't come from France or England. You could never be a Crusader." Mounir's response is indicative of his confusion over identity. "Are you sure? He asked with a sadness that misted his eyes, Then what am I going to become?"[25] The sadness in Mounir's eyes expresses disorientation and fear that speak of the loss of identity and historical memory as the legacies of colonialism.

The novel narrates the Mediterranean torn apart by civil wars but also by a traditionally male culture of honour and shame. The Mediterranean appears at times as border that defines the zone of conflict, when the narrator observes,

> From the east to the Mediterranean, tanks come to continue the work of crushing Life. The circles of oppression have also become circles of repression. Marie-Rose is not alone in her death. Second by second the inhabitants of this city that were her comrades fall. Where the tanks stop, planes take over.

At other times, it appears in one of its cultural manifestations,

> This city is like a great suffering being, too mad, too overcharged, broken now, gutted, and raped like those girls raped by thirty or forty militia men, and are now mad and in asylums because their families, Mediterranean to the end, would rather hide than cure …/but how does one cure the memory?.[26]

The militiamen argue that the violence is for a good cause; it is necessary to establish some form of order. "We want them [the children] to see what happens to traitors. [...] They'll have to see with their own eyes what's going to happen to her. They must learn so that later they won't get any ideas about rebellion. You never know, nowadays, even deaf-mutes could become subversives."[27] One of the captors, Fouad, wants the children to see Marie-Rose being murdered because it will teach them a lesson.

In her analysis of the novel, scholar Maya Aghasi observes that "seeing is a necessary pedagogical tool used to exhibit power in action, and to make those who witness this power at work submissive, docile, and accepting of the systems, values, and terms of those exercising it. In the case of this exhibition of power, the main thing the students are being taught through sight is (one version of) national identity."[28] The theatricality of the staged execution, as she observes, points to the expression of national identity in terms of a binary structure of spectators and actors, of activity and passivity, where the students

Colourless Knickknacks (After Fanon) 57

see with their own eyes what can happen when someone rebels to the rules. "Seeing, in this context," Aghasi continues, "becomes a nationalized, unchallengeable, privileged subject position, and structurally resembles a dramatic, theatrical performance." The performance of violence reaffirms and confirms the bond of belonging, and the necessity of protecting this familial bond through murder, essentially by forming a community of violence.

Standing with the Palestinians, the protagonist of Adnan's novel is also standing for a world which has seen the abolition of sectarianism; a world in which bonds are established through "affiliation" rather than "filiation." Marie Rose has renounced not only her belonging to the clan but also her role as appendage to men: "She breaks on the territory of their imagination like a tidal wave. She rouses in their memories the oldest litanies of curses."[29] Marie Rose was a woman who had rebelled and who was punished with death: "She was, they admit, a worthy prey, though they don't consider her a museum piece, real booty, an exemplary catch. She was a woman, an imprudent woman, gone over to the enemy and mixing in politics...."[30] Her transgression of religious, gender, and ethnic lines—as a Christian, a woman, and a Lebanese who is sexually and politically involved with the Palestinians—subverts the dichotomy of self and other; it cracks the lines of belonging and challenges the division of the city according to ethnic, religious, and national lines.

Yet, the act that annihilates her simultaneously reveals the precariousness of such a sacrifice. Harrison notes that here death is also "an allegory for the dismemberment of the nation, and for the internal divisions that her transgression reveals as simultaneously fatal and fantasmagorical."[31] The transgression of the boundary exposes the vulnerability and the mechanism that control that very border of separation, the myth of the nation, and the colonial compartmentalisation of societal interests. In the face of the sense of powerlessness, Marie Rose refuses to give in to the motives of this violence.

She refuses to choose between two alternatives, to be in or out of her community; she refuses the logic of separation that divides between friends and enemies. Her refusal exposes the vulnerability of the Christian militias' ideology, the senselessness of their sense of superiority towards Arabs, and puts a whole ideological system into crisis. Adnan's portrait of Marie Rose presents a woman who has refused to bend to this deadly logic, and she is celebrated in her uncompromising determination and rebellion.

In this novel, Adnan interrogates language, the kind of language that can express this sense of loss of memory and the cruelty of the violence, and asks how memory can be cured and how to live with the memory of the traumatic events. It is a question of imagination, of finding a language adequate to express the memory without reproducing its violence, and imagining what other stories can be told from the perspective of those who refuse to bend to the deadly logic of death.

Marie Rose is celebrated by Adnan in its refusal of sectarian violence and as a possibility of imagining other constellations and solidarities and chosen

58 *Imagination Besieged*

families. It memorialises and records the memory of Marie Rose in the form of fiction, offering a different viewpoint of the facts. Adnan's Sitt Marie Rose is not an escape into a fantastic and mythological world in which the Mediterranean appears as a romantic landscape or a nostalgic place of memory. On the contrary, the Mediterranean is seen in all its brutality and the structural violence that crosses and traverses its shores.

The novel, as is the case of other Adnan's works, observes and reckons with the immediate violence of the present of war: religious and political sectarian and clan-like mentalities, corruptions, divisions, sexism, and a culture of honour and shame which strangles and oppresses. Against this background of Mediterranean violence, Adnan's poetic realism problematises the loss of life, memory, and language in the aftermath of colonialism. Sitt Marie Rose offers a more realistic portrait of what it means to live in the oppressive environment of the Mediterranean torn apart by colonialism and wars as a woman. Despite her tragic end, she represents a glimpse of hope in the otherwise senseless violence and hopeless cruelty perpetrated during the civil war. She is a figure of defiance and love.

In the present Mediterranean devastated by war, economic and social crises, and environmental catastrophes, Adnan's novel remains of great relevance, among other reasons, for the way it problematises any form of identity and identitarian and nationalistic discourse that serves the political ends of those in power. Marie Rose is also the expression of a possible solidarity, one that is and is not particularly or specifically "Mediterranean" because it defies borders.

It is the possible alliance of solidarities that brings together the stories of the women narrated by Nando Primerano's book *Ci sono storie di donne* [*There are women's stories...*][32] published by Città del Sole edition, Reggio Calabria. In a series of literary portraits, Primerano brings together a surprising constellation of women. He tells the stories of Vera Cavallaro, or Swee Chai Ang, Leyla Zana, and Anna Gaggio, among others, rebellious women who, through their daily commitment and work, have fought for collective liberation. He tells of Swee Chai Ang, a Singaporean doctor who witnessed first-hand the massacre of Sabra and Chatila and who, as we are told, goes back every year to the camp to pay tribute to the Palestinians who lost their lives murdered by the Zionist entity and their proxies, the Lebanese Christian militias. Or Vera Cavallaro, the daughter of Paquale Cavallaro, who organised the revolt which led to the formation of a temporary autonomous zone in Caulonia, on the eastern side of Calabria, called "The red republic of Caulonia."

Primero's book, divided into seventeen chapters, each one telling the story of a woman, is in fact a choral portrait and the author's attempt at linking different stories through what these women engender, their solidarity and commitment to collective liberation. An attempt, as the author himself described it, to shed light on the "hidden lives whose merits have been ignored

Colourless Knickknacks (After Fanon)   59

or claimed by others," and prevent their stories, as that of Adnan's, from falling into oblivion. The book, besides literary merits, is the record of lives lived in an ethos of transnational anti-imperialist solidarity.

In "Etel Adnan's Transcolonial Mediterranean," Olivia Harrison speaks of "transcolonial Mediterranean," that is, a site of (neo)colonial subjugation and at the same time of anti-(neo)colonial resistance: "a region that has been and is built by overlapping forms of imperial domination and at the same time by Southern alliances—South beyond its own shores." [33] The Mediterranean becomes, again in Harrison's words, a "decolonial literary topos," which includes the Lebanese civil war, the Palestinian, the battles of the Native Americans, and also the movement of the 1960s and 1970s against the war in Vietnam.

In their different ways, both Adnan's work of fiction and Primerano's short stories portray women who have defied the status quo and that required the reproduction of violence. Both works are moved by a desire to tell and celebrate the untold stories of women's quotidian resistance to oppression, and preserve their memories for future generations.

Notes

1 Franz Fanon, "Concerning Violence" in *The Wretched of the Earth*, 1961.

2 Albert Camus and Arthur Goldhammer, *Algerian Chronicles* (Cambridge, MA: The Belknap Press of Harvard University Press, 2013).

3 Carl Rommel and Joseph John Viscomi, "Introduction: Locating the Mediterranean" in *Locating the Mediterranean: Connections and Separations across Space and Time*, edited by Carl Rommel and Joseph J. Viscomi (Helsinki: Helsinki University Press, 2022), 1–29.

4 Roberto Dainotto, "Asimmetrie Mediterranee: Etica e mare nostrum," *NAE, 3*, 3–18, 2003.

5 Franz Fanon, *The Wretched of the Earth*, p. 43.

6 Franz Fanon, *The Wretched of the Earth*, p. 43.

7 This critical perspective continues to inform postcolonial and cultural studies (see, for example, Dobie, 2014; Elhariry and Talbayev, 2018; Proglio et al., 2020; Smythe, 2018; Yashin, 2014). Post-colonial studies applied to the Mediterranean perspective therefore question the categories that have long dominated the vision of scholars of the Mediterranean.

8 See Fernand Braudel, *The Mediterranean and the Mediterranean World in the Age of Philip II Volume I* (University of California Press, 2003). David Abulafia, *The Great Sea. A Human History of the Mediterranean*, Allen Lane edition, 2011. Edmund Burke, "The Mediterranean of Modernity: The Long Duree Perspective," *The Making of the Modern Mediterranean: Views from the South* (Berkeley: University of California Press, 2019). Alessandra Di Maio, "Il mediterraneo nero: Rotte dei migranti nel millennio globale," in *La Città Cosmopolita*, edited by Giulia de Spuches, 2012, 143–163. Palermo: Palumbo Editore. Claudio Fogu, *The Fishing Net and the Spider Web: Mediterranean Imaginaries and the Making of Italians* (Basingstoke: Palgrave Macmillan, 2020). Peregrine Horden and Nicholas Purcell, *The Corrupting Sea: A Study of Mediterranean History* (WILEY Blackwell, 2020). Ilham Khury Makdisi, *The Eastern Mediterranean and the Making of*

60 *Imagination Besieged*

Global Radicalism, 1860–1914 (University of California Press, 2013). Matvejević, Predrag, *Breviario Mediterraneo*. Trans. by Silvio Ferrari. Pref. Claudio Magris (Milan: Garzanti, 2004) (revised and expanded edition). [*Mediteranski Brevijar*. Zagabria: Grafički zavod Hrvatske, 1987.] [*Mediterranean. A Cultural Landscape*. Trans. by Michael Henry Heim (Berkeley: University of California Press, 1999)] Judlirh E. Tucker, *The Making of the Modern Mediterranean. Views from the South* (University of California Press, 2019).

9 It means to link apparently distinct events together: the context of decolonisation, the new relationship of the European Community with the Arab-Islamic Mediterranean countries, the occupation of Historic Palestine, the energy crisis of 1973, as well as the more recent Euro-Arab dialogue, the process of Europe's Mediterranean policy, the Euro-Mediterranean Partnership of 1995, European positions and participation in military interventions in countries of the Arab and Islamic world, and the most recent deadly migratory crisis.

10 Tiziana Terranova and Iain Chambers, "Technology, Postcoloniality, and the Mediterranean," e-flux journal, Issue #123, December 2021. Available through: https://www.e-flux.com/journal/123/436918/technology-postcoloniality-and-the-mediterranean/

11 Tiziana Terranova and Iain Chambers, "Technology, Postcoloniality, and the Mediterranean," e-flux journal, Issue #123, December 2021. Available through: https://www.e-flux.com/journal/123/436918/technology-postcoloniality-and-the-mediterranean/

12 Tiziana Terranova and Iain Chambers, "Technology, Postcoloniality, and the Mediterranean," e-flux journal, Issue #123, December 2021. Available through: https://www.e-flux.com/journal/123/436918/technology-postcoloniality-and-the-mediterranean/

13 Schäfer, I., The Cultural Dimension of the Euro-Mediterranean Partnership: A Critical Review of the First Decade of Intercultural Cooperation. *History and Anthropology, 18*(3), 333–352, 2007.

14 In Denise Ferreira da Silva's conception, the idea of cultural difference entails the "production of human collectives as 'strangers' with fixed and irreconcilable moral attributes."

15 Iain Chambers and Marta Cariello, *La Questione Mediterranea* (Mondadori, 2019).

16 Iain Chambers and Marta Cariello, "The Mediterranean Question: Thinking with the Diver," *Journal of Mediterranean Knowledge-JMK, 5*(1), 141–149, 2020.

17 Iain Chambers and Marta Cariello, "The Mediterranean Question: Thinking with the Diver," *Journal of Mediterranean Knowledge-JMK, 5*(1), 141–149, 2020.

18 Etel Adnan, *Sitt Marie Rose* (trans. Georgina Kleege) (Sausalito, CA: Post-Apollo Press, 1982).

19 https://www.sciencespo.fr/mass-violence-war-massacre-resistance/fr/document/historiography-and-memory-lebanese-civil-war.html

20 P. 13.

21 P. 37.

22 P. 55.

23 P. 68.

24 P. 48.

25 P. 48.

26 P. 21.

27 P. 61.

28 Maya Aghasi, "Pedagogy of an Execution: National Identity As a Gendered Structure of Vision in Etel Adnan's Sitt Marie Rose," in *Identity and Conflict in the Middle East and Its Diasporic Cultures*, edited by Mazen Naous (Balamand: Publications of the University of Balamand, 2016).

29 Adnan, p. 89.
30 P. 61.
31 Olivia C. Harrison, "Resistances of Literature: Strategies of Narrative Affiliation in Etel Adnan's *Sitt Marie Rose*," in *Postcolonial Text*, 5(1), 2009. Pdf available through: https://www.postcolonial.org/index.php/pct/article/view/1003/963
32 Nando Primerano, *Ci sono storie di donne…*, (Reggio Calabria: Città del Sole edizioni, 2011).
33 Harrison (2018: 202).

6 Living with Ruins

For most of my adult life, I have sought an escape from the "ruins"—of my village, of my wrecked region, of Italian politics—in search of a future of socio-economic mobility and opportunities elsewhere. I did not know that this "elsewhere," however, was precisely the ruins I could not free myself from; that "elsewhere" was a possibility continually postponed, to another time, another occasion, another place, after the next crisis. The ruins have followed me everywhere—in the life "left" behind in Calabria, as much as in the cities I moved to, where post-industrial traces of failed promises of progress made room for the creativity industry and precarious cultural workers like me. The ruins became the dominant scenario of an entire era—in the destruction caused by environmental catastrophes and wars, crises that have plagued all the parts of the Mediterranean—from Syria, Libya, Tunisia, Morocco, to Palestine or Lebanon.

In this essay, I reflect on "ruins" both as a material artefact that participates in the construction of national narratives and as the traces of a process that lays out the contours of precarious violent environment. I am here specifically interested in the role of ruins in shaping national imaginaries and, at the same time, becoming active agents in shaping the politics of slow violence. Ruins too are about viewpoints: if the Northern European intellectuals saw in the ancient ruins of the Southern Italy and Greece evidence of ancient grandeur and splendour, the Southern intellectuals, such as Alvaro or Fortunati, tell us of a different type of ruins, produced by natural catastrophes but also the ruinous social conditions that have shaped the region and the lives of Southern Italians when the Italian nation came into being. For them, the obsession with the ancient amounts to rhetorics feeding the dreams of grandeurs of local intellectuals.

·

If one looks beyond the beautiful beaches and the crystalline waters of the Mediterranean Sea, the ruins of Saracene's watchtowers, Greek and Roman temples, and medieval castles, Calabria is a landscape of destruction: villages, towns, and cities, as the Italian-Senegalese rapper F.U.L.A. sings, resemble

DOI: 10.4324/9781003492634-7

Living with Ruins 63

"pits for the lasts and the outcasts." Alvaro describes this landscape of ruins in the story of Melusina as follows: "The town is rapidly falling apart, the deserted squares and streets are amplified by the meanders that open up in the collapsing houses… the roofs and floors in the kitchens and stables collapse with every rain… the erratic plants have taken refuge on the crests of the walls freed from the roofs…on the collapsed windowsills."[1] The village of Alvaro's story tells of the catastrophic environmental catastrophes that led, at the turn of the twentieth century, to the abandonment of entire areas and to mass migration first towards the coast and later to other countries and continents. And if Alvaro limits itself to observe the ruins of small villages, Giustino Fortunati goes a step further and describes the entirety of Calabria as a "sfaciume pendulo sul mare" ("rubbles hanging over the sea"), making reference to the notoriously unstable hydrogeological structure of the region, which literally geographically "leans over the sea."

On the one hand, the Imperial expansion requires the mobilisation of a national narrative based on material evidence and legitimation in the disciplines of, among others, archaeology and anthropology. On the other hand, what the process of modernisation effectively meant was the creation of more ruins through urbanisation, industrialisation, mass-migration, the pollution of the waters and of the territory, and the destruction of the entire socio-ecological ecosystem.

The identity of the southerner, according to anthropologist Vito Teti, is thus the fruit of a complex geography and history, defined by earthquakes, floods, plague, cholera, and other cataclysms that have profoundly defined the life, stories, mentality, cultures, and identity of populations who lived in conditions of perpetual insecurity and precariousness. What kind of stories do the "ruins" of this "Mediterranean" torn apart by continuous violence tell? At the time of rising ethnocentric nationalisms across Europe, if culture does not want to retreat into the past, what does it mean, in the context of Mediterranean artistic and cultural production, to deal with, or take care of the ruins of the past; ruins that exist in proximity and relation to the ruinous conditions in which communities in Southern Italy live, amid social, economic, and cultural emergencies?

The truth, Alvaro writes, is that "the poor worker flees into migration and the intellectual flees into the past. Rhetoric, yes, that is national." And while Alvaro and Fortunato were trying to give a realistic portrait of the material conditions that gave form to "Calabrian" identity, many local intellectuals were given the task to invent foundational myths and mythical places that would attest to the "noble" origins of otherwise poor and illiterate Calabrians. It was a national project with an aspiration to create a national community that would recognise itself in a common language and an image of cultural and social unity. Alvaro again comments,

From the Greeks, the southerners have taken their character of mythomaniacs. And they invent fables about their life that in reality is unadorned.

64 *Imagination Besieged*

Those like me who deal with describing their wills and needs are accused of revealing the plagues and miseries, while the landscape, they say, is so beautiful.[2]

With irony, he observes that some Calabrian intellectuals preferred to represent Calabria as a mythical place, inventing fables about its grandeur and ancient splendour, rather than to deal with the realities of a region plagued by poverty, corruption, and misgovernance. Classical ruins, as Alvaro argues, became opportunities for speculation and cultural politics that promoted national propaganda.

It was part of the project of nationalisation that was to turn a fragmented territory into a community with a shared past. "*Fatta l'Italia, bisogna fare gl'italiani.*" We have made Italy; now we must make Italians the most famous maxim in the mythology of Italian unification (1860). In *The Fishing Net*, Claudio Fogu observes that the Italian case constitutes an anomaly in the landscape of European nation-building since the nation (Italy) was constructed before there existed an "imagined community" of people who shared a language and a culture. For centuries, Italians had been made abroad rather than at home, in the images and descriptions by both others and by themselves.

When Italy became a nation, the "cultural identity" born in the various diasporas became the bricks for the newly born nation. But the idea that the Italians had to be made after unification meant that the "South" was to be predicated on "the extraction of the ex-Kingdom of the Two Sicilies from the imagined community of the Mediterranean continent to which it had belonged for centuries."[3] An example of this attempt is documented by researcher Ilaria Giglioli in the context of Southern Italian migration to Tunisia.

During the second half of the nineteenth century, precariousness, the absence of jobs, and difficult economic conditions led many Southerners to immigrate for work to Tunisia, thanks to its geographical proximity. The different communities lived in relative peace until Tunisia became a French protectorate. It was then that, moved by nationalist and imperial desires, the Italian and French elites began to see in the southerners an opportunity to contrast the mounting indigenous rebellion against the colonisers. Thus, the same sources that had once described Calabrians and Sicilians as primitive and uncivilised also spoke of them as "good workers, resistant to heat, and therefore a precious aid to French colonization." Giglioli observes, "For the Sicilians to be a full support to Italian or French ambitions on Tunisia, this population had to be 'modernized,' civilized and made into national subjects (French or Italian)."[4]

The French protectorate in Tunisia was a place of racialising differentiation between two populations—the Tunisian and the Sicilian and Calabrian (or the new Italians), and which served the imperial purpose of defining the boundaries of being and belonging to Europe. Southerners thus learned the myth of "Latinity" and their own Italian identity in a propaganda campaign

Living with Ruins   65

that became the pretext to undermine and essentially divide the common interests of Tunisian and Southern-Italian workers. Through the ideology of nationalism and white supremacy, a highly romanticised version of history was invented, which affirmed European supremacy over North Africa, and the ideals of Christian humanism against the "backward muslim" to justify colonial violence and interrupt the possibilities of solidarity among the workers against their common "enemy"—the colonialist, landowner, and factory owner.

In the same way that Sicilians and Calabrians had to be made Italians abroad, Calabrians inside Italy had to provide with a basic education that would instil in them a patriotic sentiment. This discourse was to be reconstructed through a re-reading of the ancient ruins. The first time I visited the Norman-Swabian castle of Squillace, I found myself in a small museum room built on the ruins of the castle and full of dusty medieval memorabilia. It was called "the warriors' room." Displayed on a large wall were a series of symbols representing the various families which had owned the land—among them the Borgias and Roger of Hauteville, who here ceded to San Bruno of Cologne the lands where the Certosa di Serra San Bruno would later be built. Nowhere is mentioned that the castle was built on other ruins, coming from the times of the Byzantine, who had lived here for over five centuries. As I walk through the rooms, I wondered what are the educational purposes and pedagogical value of these kinds of museum display, where history is reduced to a list of dates, names, and standards of powerful lords and barons. What kind of cultural policy is pursued? The museum of the castle is itself a ruin, a wreck of a fantasy, that of the nation and of national identity.

•

At the crossroads of ideological, imperialistic interests and mythical and religious narratives, during the nineteenth century and part of the twentieth century, ancient ruins become national "archaeological heritage," material evidence of the veracity and therefore legitimacy of ancient myths, biblical stories, and political and territorial claims. In *The Nation and Its Ruins: Antiquity, Archaeology, and National Imagination in Greece*, Yannis Hamilakis insists that, in the context of modern Greece, "archaeology as a discipline, as a set of principles, devices, methods, and practices, creates its object of study, from existing and real, past material traces"[5] in the same way that nationalism produced the entity and identity that gives it meaning and purpose, the nation.

In this volume, Hamilakis focuses on nationalism as an everyday ideology and looks at the social lives of the ruins in the context of Greek nationalist project and popular imagination. To understand the materiality of the past and how it has shaped national imagination Hamilakis refers, among others, to the controversy surrounding the Elgin Marbles—a collection of artefacts mostly from the Parthenon taken in the beginning of the nineteenth century by Lord Elgin and housed at the British Museum. Their ownership is highly contested

66 *Imagination Besieged*

by both the Greek government and the museum authorities. This has been elevated to an issue of "national importance" for most Greeks, and the return of the marbles has been a "national goal" for every Greek government since the early 1980s. The Parthenon marbles are significant not simply because of their symbolic role in the official narrative of nationhood and historical continuity between classical and modern Greek culture. But, as Hamilakis argues, it stands for the sum of ancient ruins in Greece and has become a personal affair for the majority of Greeks, who see the marble as the basis for a sense of continuity and community.

Western Hellenism was the form that colonisation took, and it was the vehicle which allowed the incorporation of this part of the Mediterranean into the Western sphere of influence. Hamilakis reminds us that material culture as a national project is not static but constantly produced and reproduced in an ongoing negotiation between different agents, groups, and interests. The antiquities of Greece were meant to be seen, experienced, and appreciated as "national artifacts." Hamilakis, together with Rafael Greenberg, has also observed that classical archaeology in the context of the "holy land" can be considered the "ground zero" of European modernity and it grew in parallel to imperial expansion and the settlement projects of Zionism.[6] The Israeli regime has long attempted to erase the non-Jewish heritage of the region and to appropriate the archaeological heritage to establish a historical connection with the Holy Land and support the idea of exclusive ownership of this land.

Hamilakis insists that in both the case of Greece and Palestine and Israel, but similar considerations can be expanded to the case of Southern Italy, as we have seen, archaeology happens at the intersection of colonial and national interests and imaginaries. Colonial archaeology turned ruins into a profitable enterprise to make the nation "modern" and heavily relied more than on the material artefacts themselves, on selective historical memory and geography.

Palestine is a significant example of the ways in which ruins and archaeological studies have served the colonial and national project of constructing "Israel." The collective called *Depth Unknown*, which has studied archaeological excavations and the architecture of occupation, observes, "since the last decades of the 19th century, Western imperial powers have deployed archaeologists and geographers to find on the ground material evidence of the stories contained in the Bible."[7] Archaeologists did not come alone, but they were accompanied by cartographers and military attachés, to "'retrive on the ground the traced of the geography of the scriptures. As a result, Arab Ottoman Palestine disappeared from the maps; Palestine was 'mapped back' onto the past that the Biblical narration described."[8]

The ancient past of the Middle East has been not only studied but also more fundamentally appropriated, incorporated into a grand narration of the origins of Imperial Western Power: rising from Mesopotamia and transferred to Egypt, Assyria, Media, Persia, the Greeks, and congealed into the Roman Empire.[9] In that sense, archaeology in the Middle East and Palestine, as

Living with Ruins 67

Margarita Díaz-Andreu (2007) writes, was an appropriative effort of "consolidation of the mythical roots of the West." This discourse on the ruins, as Yannis Hamilakis and Claudio Fogu through colonial archaeology, paradoxically pushed Greece and Southern Italy away from their belonging to the Mediterranean, towards an imagined white Westerner European Judeo-Christian cultural community.

•

If, on the one hand, it is crucial to understand how the ruins participate in and are instrumentalised in nationalistic discourse, as Hamilakis and others do, in recent years, the discussion on ruins has shifted from the material artefact to the ways in which ruins actively partake in the construction of the politics of the present. Ruins in this sense are not dead-matter, but agent of a process of what Ann Stoler[10] calls "ruination," and that she describes as "a corrosive process that weighs on the future and shapes the present."[11]

It is what people are "left with" rather than what is memorialised in the ruins. Stoler argues that the ruination of capitalist, colonial and imperial violence generates physical destruction, emotional breakdowns, gutted infrastructures, and toxicities of the soul and soil. While the action that led to the process of decay and rotting seems to disappear, the rot actually remains "long after the colonial officials have returned 'home' and anxious white settlers have relinquished hold on what was never theirs, are gone." To think with the ruins presupposes then an intellectual, poetic, and political engagement with the present, rather than a melancholic musing at an atemporal and ahistorical idea of the past and its decontextualised preservation.

It is to attend to "their reappropriations and strategic and active positioning within the politics of the present."[12] In this sense, ruination does not assume that something belongs to a past we're done with, but it forces us to deal with its reverberations in the present. It offers a critical vantage point and redirects the engagement with ruins "elsewhere," to the ways in which people inhabit ruins.

While Stoler focuses on the larger structural dimension of ruination, I here want to focus on the loss of identity and the psycho-affective responses to living with ruins in the specific context of Calabria, in the *long-durée* of crises, disasters, catastrophes, and social abandonment that characterise the region. In one of the scenes from the movie by Carlo Carlei entitled *La Corsa dell'Innocente* [Flight of the Innocent] (1992), a young 10-year-old Calabrian boy, Vito, runs for his life as members of a rival 'ndrangheta family try to kill him. Vito's family lives off the kidnapping of children of the wealthy people. All the components of his family have been murdered, killed by an internal *faida*.

Vito runs through the desolate industrial ruins of the *Liquichimica Biosintesi* in Saline Ioniche, Reggio Calabria. He runs through the abandoned architecture, the gigantic rusty metal structures, on the concrete pavement infested

68 *Imagination Besieged*

by wild plants; he passes a pond of dirty greenish water and runs through the metal bridges that connect the different parts of an industrial complex, which extends for 700 thousand square meters on the Calabrian eastern coast. The area where Liquichimica was built was occupied by a disused salt mine, but also by orange groves and bergamot plantations. Its construction began in the early 1970s when the Italian government allocated 1,300 billion lire to support a series of industrial investments that were supposed to create thousands of jobs in Calabria and Sicily and calm the protests of the so-called "Reggio riots."[13]

The factory was meant to produce bioproteins,[14] which a few months before the opening, were declared dangerous and carcinogenic by the Higher Institute of Health. Meanwhile, 'ndrangheta took possession of the area and continued to exploit the infrastructure. The port of Saline Joniche became a landing point for drug trafficking. Vito arrives at what is probably one of those landing points, a metal platform protruding into the sea. He sits there and stares at the sea.

The choice of filming inside the Liquichimica is suggestive. The desolate landscape of the dismissed factory speaks of an environment of ruins and abandonment that is all around Vito, and that defines as much his life and as the destiny of his Calabria. He gazes into the sea melancholically. He has lost his family. His entire world is being physically and emotionally destroyed. He feels stuck and can't shake away his fears now that he is alone, the ruins of the Liquichimica, which stands there as a monument to the failure of progress. A monument to the failure of Italian politics to respond to the grievances of the Calabrian communities, their needs, desires, and expectations.

The ruins of the Liquichimica are emblematic of the failure of modernisation and the devastating effects on the local population, on their ability to imagine a future for themselves. 'Ndrangheta thrives precisely where the failures of the nation and of national politics have failed to solve the disparities between the two parts of the country. In the film, the ruins construct the identity of Vito, and by extension of Calabria, as a reality characterised by precarity and the impossibility of imagining alternative futures. In the film, Vito is stuck in the same narrative of the Calabrian 'ndrangheta man, in the same way that Calabria itself is stuck either in the myth of an ancient past or in a present of emergencies and destruction. And yet, that doesn't mean that Vito doesn't try to change something. How to call this impulse to live, to run away (because in the film we often see Vito running)?

More recently, filmmaker Jonas Carpignano has attempted to capture through the lens' eye the constellation of degradation and the environment of violence in which Calabrians and minorities coexist, their alienation and sense of confinement within this landscape of ruins. In *A' Cambra*, Carpignango narrates the coming of age of a young Roma boy, Pio, who, now that his father and brother are in jail, can aspire to become someone. It tells of his entry into the adult world—in that community where, as his grandfather tells him, "t's us

Living with Ruins 69

against the world." Carpignano carefully juxtaposes the way the film's Roma characters are treated by the Italians ("You black piece of shit," says one) with that community's own racism (the older Amatos talk about how scared and disgusted they are by the neighbouring "Africans").

However, unlike Marie Rose in Etel Adnan's story, who decides to rebel to her community, Pio eventually betrays his friendship with the "maroccan guy," an African man who came here as a refugee and now is exploited working in the field, to show his loyalty to the "clan." This dynamic makes for a considered study of racial tensions among outsiders. "The strength of the community is also its limit"—says Carpignano—"they don't betray each other and will never betray each other, but this also penalises them in their relationships with the outside world."[15]

A "Ciambra," which gives the name to the film, is a neighbourhood in Gioia Tauro home to a large community of Roma. It is, like Liquichimica, another ruin, the failed housing project that was supposed to integrate, but created further marginalisation and a degraded living environment. In this Calabria in which living among the ruins feels very much like a prison, Pio and Vito seem to share a similar already written destiny that ties them to their respective communities. They both embody the possibilities of change, as they both want to exit the rules and codes imposed by their familial ties–Vito by telling the truth to the family of the kidnapped child, Pio by becoming friend with the African man. However, in both cases, the family ties remain too strong to come undone. They're stuck. They have been abandoned by a failing social and political system which does not seem interested in solving simple problems and supporting them through forms of transformative justice. This sense of abandonment contrasts with the preservation of the ruins that local administrations seem so obsessed with. But in a strange way, they're both stuck in and debilitating environment of violence that delimits the possibilities of a different imagination.

Notes

1 Corrado Alvaro, "Ritratto di Melusina," in L'Amata alla finestra. Introduzione di Walter Pedullà, bibliografia di Massimo Onofri; I grandi tascabili 347, Milano Bompiani, fifth edition (1994).
2 Corrado Alvaro, *Gente in Aspromonte* (Milano: Garzanti, 2017).
3 Corrado Alvaro, *Gente in Aspromonte* (Milano: Garzanti, 2017), 3.
4 Ilaria Giglioli, "Unmaking the Mediterranean Border. Mediterraneanism, Colonial Mobilities and Postcolonial Migration," *Tesi di dottorato* (University of California Berkeley, 2018). Available through: https://digitalassets.lib.berkeley.edu/etd/ucb/text/Giglioli_berkeley_0028E_17932.pdf
5 Yannis Hamilakis, *The Nation and Its Ruins: Antiquity, Archaeology, and National Imagination in Greece* (Oxford University Press, 2009).
6 See: Yannis Hamilakis and Rafael Greenberg, *Modernity's Sacred Ruins: Colonialism, Archaeology, and the National Imagination in Greece and Israel* (2021). Available through: https://www.bsa.ac.uk/videos/yannis-hamilakis-

70 *Imagination Besieged*

rafael-greenberg-modernitys-sacred-ruins-colonialism-archaeology-and-the-national-imagination-in-greece-and-israel/

7 *Depth Unknown* website. Available through: https://depthunknown.com/

8 Abu El-Haj, N. *Facts on the Ground: Archaeological Practice and Territorial Self-fashioning in Israeli Society* (Chicago, IL: The University of Chicago Press, 2002).

9 See Liverani, M., "Imperialism," *Archaeologies of the Middle East. Critical Perspectives*, edited by Pollock, S. and Bernbeck, R. (Oxford: Blackwell, 2005), 223–243.

10 Ann Stoler, *"The Rot Remains": From Ruins to Ruination* (2013).

11 Ann Stoler, *"The Rot Remains": From Ruins to Ruination* (2013).

12 Ann Stoler, *"The Rot Remains": From Ruins to Ruination* (2013).

13 A series of violent protests followed the decision to identify Catanzaro, and not Reggio Calabria, as the regional capital. For eight months there were riots, attacks, and clashes with the police, with six deaths and dozens injured. In 1970, the city of Reggio Calabria revolted in a siege that lasted for more than six months, between July 1970 and February 1971. Several hundred years of frustration re-emerged to be expressed anew. The event that sparked the insurrection was the Italian government's decision to intervene in the regional politics. What was narrated as a disproportioned response to a futile motivation was, however, a discontent and frustration that had deep roots in the condition of poverty and exploitation of people living in this region, who were simply not listened to. An article of the Milan section of the International Situationists published in the same year, 1970, described the revolts in this manner: in this new period of crisis, Reggio Calabria is the first example of a town (at the heart of capitalist exploitation) that has fought for more than three months and organised itself. Isolated by a general wildcat strike and an undeclared state of siege, the town has bravely defended the freedom it has won, firing without restraint on the police forces and setting up barricades connected to high-voltage electricity. See, https://libcom.org/history/workers-italy-revolt-reggio-calabria.

14 Bioproteins are proteins produced from substances derived from petroleum that in theory would have served as animal feed. The patent for bioproteins was Russian, and Liquichimica was designed on the model of a similar plant built in Gorky, a city now known as Nizhny Novgorod, just over 400 kilometres east of Moscow. According to the intentions of the experts who studied this market at the time, bioproteins would have replaced the normal cycle of land-forage-meat with the one called petroleum-bioproteins-meat.

15 Leonardo Goi, "Us Against the World: Jonas Carpignano's Calabrian Trilogy," in MUBI, 2022. Available through: https://mubi.com/en/notebook/posts/us-against-the-world-jonas-carpignano-s-calabrian-trilogy

7 The Death Deal

In the 1980s and 1990s, 'Ndrangheta and other criminal organisations across the Mediterranean borders were trading. Their trade consisted in sinking ships transporting highly toxic waste. It was called by the newspaper *As-Safi*, the "death deal." This deadly deal linked countries in the Global South receiving toxic waste coming from the Global North, in a geography of toxicities[1] that extended well beyond the Mediterranean, in an intricate network of "investors," involving both state and private companies, mafia, politicians, and greedy shipowners happy to make extra-profit from the payment of insurance prizes. "Garbage is gold,"[2] commented Mafia boss Nunzio Perrella, the so-called "King of Waste," describing to Napoli prosecutors in 1992 that the business of rubbish and toxic waste was more profitable and less risky than the drug trade.

Cunsky, Rigel, Yvonne A, Voriais Sparadis, Mikigan, Marylijoan, Aouxum, Monika, and the Jolly Rosso: These ships disappeared with their toxic content at several locations in the central and southern Mediterranean; these include locations in Capo Spartivento,[3] off the coasts of Calabria, as well as the coasts of Greece, Tunisia, Lebanon, Sierra Leone, and Somalia.[4] When some of them arrive at their destination, their content was stored in quarries, illegal landfills, warehouses, or disposal on unsuitable land or beyond the community borders.

The sinking ships are the material remnants of certain politics of "slow violence"—following Bob Nixon's definition, a violence which happens "gradually and out of sight, a violence of delayed destruction that is dispersed across time and space, an attritional violence that is typically not viewed as violence at all"[5]. Crises that only seem to produce more crises and more opportunities for exploitation, which in turns produces the degradation of the social and environmental life.

Past the dramatic events, who and what are people left with? How do they inhabit these toxic geographies? From studies conducted by the Smaurn (Sistema Monitoraggio Ambientale Reti Neurali), the area of Villa S. Giovanni is the most polluted in Calabria, with high percentages of toxic substances released in the air. Epidemiological data from Campania indicates that there might be a causal relationship between illegal dumping of toxic substances

DOI: 10.4324/9781003492634-8

72   *Imagination Besieged*

and incidence of cancer.[6] Similarly, studies conducted in Somalia, where the mafia has dumped hazardous waste on large scale, have shown a correlation between the events and the increase in cancer rates since 1993.[7] And yet, these "accidents" were supposed to disappear, like their witnesses, like the interests that are supposed to cover.

These shipwrecks speak to the environmental degradation produced by persistent violence and disregard for some lives deemed less valuable than others.[8] They conceal the impact, unquantified because not verified until now, of those environmental crimes on people's livelihood and ability to face the challenges of climate change in the present. The dissemination of toxicity is slow and unspectacular, yet violent and lethal; it produces cancers, physical and psychological malformations, contaminates water and land, and it exterminates animals and plants and pollutes the sea. The effects of such events are far-reaching. In an article on The Cairo Observer, Garret Barnwell and Savo Heleta warn of the effects of climate change-related displacement, which, as they write, "will negatively impact the Global South the most.[...] A combination of environmental degradation, violence, physical destruction, displacement, and mental health challenges and traumas in conflict zones and other fragile settings will reduce the ability of many people and communities to adapt to climate change, cope, and survive. [...]."[9]

Climatologists have argued that the scarcity of water and changes in climate are factors that, for instance, precipitated the civil war in Syria. Between 2007 and 2010, the wheat crop in North-eastern Syria suffered a "complete failure" in the most severe three-year drought on record, Kelley said. "That was unprecedented."[10] Author and researcher Sintia Issa[11] opens her study of infrastructural failures and the politics of slow death in the context of Lebanon garbage politics with a conversation she had with a fisherman from Dora, outside North of Beirut, who lamented that the sea is dead and there is nothing left to fish. For the fishermen, this is related to the Lebanese government's decision to dump millions of tons of waste from the civil war in and around Beirut and Mount Lebanon.

In the 1990s, the Beiruti fishermen organised against the government's decision to turn the land around the fishing port into a mount of trash. But nothing could stop the plan. The Lebanese government saw the processing of garbage and waste from the civil war as an opportunity for new investment and speculation. Most of the dumpsters and of the materials for the construction of the Beirut waterfront, for instance, come from the recycling of unusable toxic waste from the war and from illicit traffics, such as the deal of the poison ships.

The point Issa is making is that the degradation of the environment is the result of crisis turned into opportunities for capitalist destruction, as the case of Lebanese and the Italian politics of garbage collecting clearly exposes—crisis that could have been solved but was wilfully left to rot, to turn into a

The Death Deal 73

disaster to be managed through "special" interventions, often led by mafia and corrupted politicians.

The tangle of interests and relations which has been partly uncovered by various investigations[12] shows the intertwined relations between illicit traffic of radioactive waste, arms trafficking, and national governments. However, what it's noticeable in the story is, on the one hand, the attempt to make the information regarding these ships and their content disappear and, on the other, the almost invisible forms and manifestations of the environmental violence brought about by the poisons released in the sea, the soil, and the air.

The "secrecy" around these shipments and the absence of accountability for the degradation of the environment raise a series of questions about the role of institutional archives and their omissions, as well as of the difficulties in telling a story full of gaps, inconsistencies, and missing information; a story that is "dangerous" to tell. How can something that is supposed to remain silent and invisible be accounted for and bring about accountability? The story of the "death deal" has been taken up by artist and poet Jessika Khazrik in her ongoing projects *The Blue Barrel Grove* (2014-ongoing) and the long poem *Mount Mound Refuse* (2016–2022).

Since 2014, Khazrik, who was raised in Beirut, has explored the implications of the events that between 1987 and 1995 led to the dumping of toxic waste off the coasts of Lebanon. In the first iteration of the TBBG, Khazrik organised a walk-through performance, *I Couldn't but Dance* (2014), around sculptural arrangements she conceived for her storytelling. She narrated the epic journey that this shipment took—travelling to Somalia, where it was refused; then to Syria, where too it was refused; to finally end its journey in Beirut, where the government accepted the toxic cargo.

In 1987, during the midst of the civil war in Lebanon, profiting from the chaotic situation, members of the Lebanese militia were paid about 22 million USD by Italian mafia groups to get rid of about 15,800 barrels and 20 containers of toxic waste.[13] Lebanese authorities did not take notice of the imported waste because the country was ravaged by the civil war. The toxic waste was dispersed on Mount Lebanon in various locations, including one near the house where the artist grew up.

When the scandal was discovered, about a year later, Lebanese Health Minister Joseph al-Hashem hired toxicologists to investigate the case. They discovered that the barrels contained industrial waste from Italy in the form of medicines, plastics, and lubricants that were all heavily contaminated. The authorities, however, decided to ignore scientific reports and even discredited some scientists and their findings. One of the scientists, Malychef, was arrested on the premise of a "false testimony" and the photo-documentation he had accumulated was never to be made public—possibly to contain the paranoia growing in the country about the "blue barrels." But when the scandal leaked to the public, the Italian

74 *Imagination Besieged*

government had to do something and promised to retrieve all the barrels. Only half, some 5,500 barrels, however, were loaded in four ships at Beirut Port in 1988/89.

Authorities in Italy have been claiming since 1989 that all the waste had been returned on board one ship, the "Jolly Rosso." But at that time, Greenpeace had learnt that three ships, loaded with Italian waste in Beirut port, never arrived in Italy, suggesting that they had dumped their deadly cargo in the Mediterranean Sea. The Jolly Rosso made it back to Italy, but it was by pure coincidence. In December 1990, the ship ran aground along the coast of Amantea, Calabria. And when it arrived at the port of Vibo, in Calabria, the book of the ship, with all the maps that trace the routes, the stops and departures from different ports, were missing. None knew the trip the ship had undertaken before running aground on the Calabrian coast, nor what the ship was carrying.

About the Jolly Rosso, the chef who was working on board in one interview comments, "I suspected that there was something in the cargo that was supposed to sink with the entire ship. [...] The ship was sunk on purpose because, among other things, it was supposed to be demolished, but whoever was supposed to demolish it did not accept it because it still had toxic residues from the previous cargo on board."[14]

Investigators and uncomfortable witnesses were intimidated or killed, like the captain Natale De Grazia, poisoned in 1995 just before he found the missed link to conclude a big investigation that would have caused an international scandal. De Grazia was following the line opened by Italian journalist Ilaria Alpi, who had uncovered, just before she and her colleague, Miran Hrovatin, were executed in 1994, the role of the Italian government, Democrazia Cristiana, the Army and the Italian and foreign secret services in the illegal trade of weapons of rich countries with poor countries in exchange for nuclear waste.

In dealing with Malychef's unpublished archive of images related to the investigation, Khazrik's work, if on the one hand discloses the deception and corruption that these events disclose, one the other hand, it asks questions about the relation between reality and fiction, about accountability, which is ultimately also a matter of who owns the "truth." The artist adopts a speculative[15] approach to deal with absences, gaps, and silences of and around the story, imagining the events of the arrival of the material, its burial, and the long and intricate journey undertook by the poison ships.

The project took the form of an autobiographical poem, set in the "haunted" forest of Shnan'ir, scenario of a growing young love and burial ground of toxic blue barrels. The poet reminisces about a day she, Little Arsonist, spent with R__O in the forest, sometime in the twenty-first century, over a decade after the blue barrels were buried in 1987. In-between an epic poem and a fable, where strange animals speak out their minds to strangers they meet on their ways, *Mount Mound Refuse* (2016) speculates, with great irony and dark

The Death Deal 75

humour, about the events of the illicit trafficking and the poisoning of Beirut's landscape by a hand of corrupted militias and politicians.

The Lebanese Forces stood beneath a hole
A route of beautiful wolves glanced at them briefly
A صياد said
"we are not a secret"
it 2it tit it
Missing Mountain blared
Black rendered blue barrel fat
Little Arsonist
"Why were wastes installed on stones?"

The Little Arsonist meets a hyena and has a conversation about filling up the mountain. The poem unfolds as a dialogical space punctuated by a series of encounters. Dialogue works through silences. And, dialogue, as Hartman suggests, can be a way of imagining the desire for something better when the desire cannot or would not be named, "a way of imagining a presence *without* the violence of presenting it."[16]

Arthritic roads
Dioxins sulking under soil
In concrete
In buildings
Reconstructions
Beirut
My parents' house
Hurling Calmly Between Dirt
AgCN
Now we knew that
These militias even feared
Music
HAH

The poem lists in a sequence all that the blue barrels are related to: the concrete, the reconstruction of Beirut, her parents' house—a list that could have as a title "the global economy of death," in which personal memories and national crises merge to create a map of the toxic relations that shape the present of Beirut. The artist imagines the events that led to the catastrophic level of toxic material buried in the soil, where toxic waste trades attest to a world that accepts the contamination of certain less industrialised places and of some bodies more than others.[17]

The Little Arsonist speculates on the arrival of the "criminal violence," and in the final stanza, she wonders whether, through poetry, through "invisible animals," and the work of imagination, she will be able to achieve some

76 *Imagination Besieged*

form of poetic justice. Tell us the truth, the poem cries, what happened to the content of those barrels?

> o you
> i <<<333 wonder
> Will i be
> As cinema toxic
> When dead and
> Buried in
> iTALLY??
> Or would
> I have
> Abolished language
> With justice and invisible
> animals.

The language of questioning disturbs the interests of those who would prefer to keep the truths secret and bury them in silence. And in speaking up, the poet works towards the horizon of abolishing language, in the sense of disturbing the existing order of thought and the presumed neutrality of language, its institutional procedures, and scholarly protocols. The final line of the poem opens the space to the possibility of poetic justice.

Issa observes that *Mount Mound Refuse*, "speculatively challenges the state's denial of this ongoing toxic exposure, first in the 1995 legal proceedings, then in a recurring narrative that frames it as a finished event, demanding that we move on."[18] The artist refuses to do so and insists on retelling the story in always new forms and iterations. In the version from 2022, the poem has acquired new stanzas in hybrid English and Italian, which add new material and details. Khazrik refers to her own long-term investigation, and the long-term, slow, and invisible impact of those toxicities as evidence of environmental crimes:

> It took me 7 years and a half to learn
> How come in 1994 in Uyoun Al Siman,
> 400 goats were found dead
> When militias dug trenches
> Filled the earth with refilled industrial drums
> *Tutte le armi sono tossiche*
> And the poison mixed with snow
> And the snow filled the well
> And from there, the goats drank
> Murder with inter-water ghosts

She has been researching the traces and effects of those poisonous substances for over a decade. Khazrik's practice has been described by scholar Sintia

The Death Deal 77

Issa, as a "slow practice" that "demands that we take a necessarily long pause to both rethink waste beyond the simplistic understanding of it as stuff to discard, and work through the messy and complex constellation in which it is produced and disposed of."[19] Issa observes that the work attempts to challenge "the climate politics of 'urgency' that disregard structural hierarchies and sweep once again under the rug the violent histories that have produced the global regime of colonization."[20] Khazrik insists on staying with "the trouble" and continuing her process of thinking with the decaying bodies of both the national and imperial states, and the possibilities that this inevitable transformation will bring to our lives, bodies, and affects.

If, in the first version, the poem works with the absences and the gaps of the story in a more speculative manner, in the new iteration, the new additional stanzas engage the politics of failure and structural violence through an openly militant language. The tone is clearly one of protest. Since 2015, when the artist started working on this research, Lebanon has been in a garbage crisis, with more than 20,000 tons of garbage flooding the streets of Beirut, and progressively sunk into a deeper crisis: widespread poverty, power cuts, fuel and medicine shortages, inflation; then in 2019, the financial crisis; and the 2020 explosion at the port of Beirut, which killed more than 200 people and obliterated parts of the city putting more strains on Lebanon's already collapsing system. The port blast produced debris which increased the generated waste and, as Human Rights Watch has observed,[21] had the potential to become another garbage emergency.

In her poem, Khazrik acknowledges how this succession of crisis has transformed not only consciousness but also very much the bodies of those exposed to the toxic materials. The poem assesses how the toxic waste has "change our mind/with cancer." The debilitation brought by cancer is not only personal but also concerns society more broadly. Cancer is presented here as a symptom of everything that is poisonous and toxic in this world and that touches each individual differently. Sickness is entangled in the history of industry and capital, carcinogenic manufacturing—a history that is structurally racist, misogynist, classist, invested in profitable inequality, and blind to the suffering it produces. It is by following the cancerogenic substances that it is possible to draw the contours of imperial connections and histories of violence.

Speculative fiction offers the poet the possibility to imagine possible futures at a moment of critical historical transformation. As Issa observes, "In the end, this inherently speculative, latent trans-aesthetic insists that the environment we know is transforming and will continue to transform."[22] If "state violence" produced "the archival traces" of the lives of the silenced, says Saidiya Hartman about her use of a speculative approach to history, "the desire and want of something better decide the contours of the telling."[23] It is by retelling and recomposing the pieces of this story that art and poetry can tell a different story; by taking the shape of a "dangerous"

78 *Imagination Besieged*

overgrowing monstrous protest poem, one that by disclosing the "secrets" of these transnational businesses, as Khazrik hopes, transforms this "death deal" into a beautifully resistant, and resisting, entanglements of transnational solidarities.

Notes

1 Jennifer Clapp, The Toxic Waste Trade with Less-industrialized Countries: Economic Linkages and Political Alliances. *Third World Quarterly, 15*(3), 1994.

2 Alessandro Iacuelli, *Le Vie Infinite Dei Rifiuti—Il Sistema Campano* (Raleigh, 2nd edn, Lulu.Com 2007), 12.

3 See Legambiente, "Le Navi dei Veleni," report. Available through: https://noecomafia.legambiente.it/le-navi-dei-veleni/; European Union Commission. Available through: https://www.europarl.europa.eu/doceo/document/E-7-2009-5516_EN.html; Alberto Maritati, La Nave dei Veleni (Il caso Cavtat, Laterza, 2021). Mihail Tremopoulos, "Shipwrecks Containing Toxic and Nuclear Waste in the Mediterranean"; Michael Leonardi, "Italy's Secret Ships of Poison" in counterpunch.org, 2009. Available through: https://www.counterpunch.org/2009/11/04/italy-s-secret-ships-of-poison/

4 Greenpeace Italy Report, "The Toxic Ships. The Italian Hub, the Mediterranean Area and Africa, June 2010. Available through: https://www.dieselduck.info/library/05%20environmental/2010%20Greenpeace%20Toxic%20Ships.pdf

5 Rob Nixon, *Slow Violence and the Environmentalism of the Poor* (Cambridge, Massachusetts, and London: Harvard University Press, 2013).

6 Available through: https://www.pjoes.com/Frog-as-Sentinel-of-Human-Cancer-Incidence-nin-Southern-Italy-s-So-Called-n-Terra,94051,0,2.html. In Italy, a dramatic example of this situation is represented by the areas of Caserta and Naples, in the Campania region. Illegal dumping and burning of waste in this region has caused immense environmental damage which seems to have severely affected the local population's health, and so these areas are called "Land of Fires."

7 Abdulkadir Egal, *Suspected Correlation between Cancer Incidence and Industrial and Nuclear Wastes in Somalia*, December 2008, online: https://www.researchgate.net/profile/Abdulkadir-Egal/publication/274250343_Suspected_Correlation_between_Cancer_Incidence_and_Industrial_and_Nuclear_Wastes_in_Somalia/links/5d272445458515c11c25e153/Suspected-Correlation-between-Cancer-Incidence-and-Industrial-and-Nuclear-Wastes-in-Somalia.pdf; Chris Milton, Somalia Used as Toxic Dumping Ground. *The Ecologist*, 2009. Available through: https://theecologist.org/2009/mar/01/somalia-used-toxic-dumping-ground.

8 See Jennifer Clapp, The Toxic Waste Trade with Less Industrialized Countries: Economic Linkages and Political Alliances. *Third World Quarterly, 15*(3), 505–518, 1994; Muawya Ahmed Hussein, Costs of Environmental Degradation: An Analysis in the Middle East and North Africa Region. *Management of Environmental Quality. An International Journal, 9*(3), 305–317, anno 2008; Rob White, Toxic Cities. Globalizing the Problem of Waste. *Social Justice, 35*(3), 113, *War, Crisis & Transition*, 107–119, 2008–09.

9 Available through: https://www.thecairoreview.com/essays/the-slow-violence-of-climate-change/

10 Colin P. Kelley, Shahrzad Mohtadi, Mark A. Cane, and Yochanan Kushnir, Climate Change in the Fertile Crescent and Implications of the Recent Syrian Drought. *PNAS Journal, 112*(11), November 2014. Available through: https://www.pnas.org/doi/10.1073/pnas.1421533112

The Death Deal   79

11 Sintia Issa, Beyond the Garbage Politics of Emergency: The Paradox of Infrastructural Failure in Beirut's Peripheries. Available through: https://worldhumanitiesreport.org/wp-content/uploads/2023/05/WHR-AR_1.UrbanImaginaries_Issa.pdf

12 Atapattu S and Gonzalez CG, "The North–South Divide in International Environmental Law: Framing the Issues" in *International Environmental Law and the Global South*, edited by Alam S, Atapattu S, Gonzalez CG, and Razzaque J (Cambridge University Press; 2015), 1–20; Atteh, SO, The Political Economy of Environmental Degradation: The Dumping of Toxic Wastes in West Africa. *The African Review: A Journal of African Politics, Development and International Affairs*, *20*(1/2), 19–38, 1993. Available through: http://www.jstor.org/stable/45341598; Gerrit Faber, International Trade and Environmental Policies. *Environmental Policy in an International Context*, *3*, 79–103, 2003.

13 See Fouad Hamdan, *Waste Trade in the Mediterranean: Toxic Attack against Lebanon. Case One: Toxics from Italy* (Green Peace Lebanon, 1996).

14 Francesco Donnici and Andrea Carni, "Jolly Rosso, la nave dei veleni e le anomalie irrisolte" in Corriere della Calabria, 2021. Available through: https://www.corrieredellacalabria.it/2021/12/14/jolly-rosso-la-nave-dei-veleni-e-le-anomalie-irrisolte/

15 "Speculative fiction includes fantasy, science fiction, and horror, but also their derivatives, hybrids, and cognate genres like the gothic, dystopia, weird fiction, post-apocalyptic fiction, ghost stories, superhero tales, alternate history, steampunk, slipstream, magic realism, fractured fairy tales, and more. …Speculative fiction is a mode of thought-experimenting that includes narratives addressed to young people and adults and operates in a variety of formats. …The term accommodates the non-mimetic genres of Western but also non-Western and indigenous literatures—especially stories narrated from the minority or alternative perspective. In all these ways, speculative fiction represents a global reaction of human creative imagination struggling to envision a possible future at the time of a major transition from local to global humanity." From Marek Oziewicz, "Speculative Fiction." *Oxford Research Encyclopedia of Literature*. 29 Mar. 2017; Accessed 18 Sep. 2024. Available through: https://oxfordre.com/literature/display/10.1093/acrefore/9780190201098.001.0001/acrefore-9780190201098-e-78

16 Irvin Hunt, "From How We Write 'Well,'" 2019. Available through: https://post45.org/2019/01/the-style-of-speculative-history/

17 Max Liboiron, "Waste Colonialism," Discard Studies, November 1, 2018. Available through: https://discardstudies.com/2018/11/01/waste-colonialism/

18 Max Liboiron, "Waste Colonialism," Discard Studies, November 1, 2018. Available through: https://discardstudies.com/2018/11/01/waste-colonialism/, p. 113.

19 Sintia Issa, "Waste You Cannot Deny: A Slow Trans-aesthetic in The Blue Barrel Grove" in *The Routledge Companion to Contemporary Art, Visual Culture, and Climate Change* (Routledge, 2021), 112.

20 Sintia Issa, "Waste You Cannot Deny: A Slow Trans-aesthetic in The Blue Barrel Grove" in *The Routledge Companion to Contemporary Art, Visual Culture, and Climate Change* (Routledge, 2021), 112.

21 Charbel Salloum, "Lebanon Risks Another Garbage Crisis." Available through: https://www.hrw.org/news/2020/09/23/lebanon-risks-another-trash-crisis.

22 Charbel Salloum, "Lebanon Risks Another Garbage Crisis." Available through: https://www.hrw.org/news/2020/09/23/lebanon-risks-another-trash-crisis, p. 116.

23 Saidiya Hartman, The Anarchy of Colored Girls Assembled in a Riotous Manner. *South Atlantic Quarterly*, 117, 465–490, July, 2018.

8 Imagination Besieged

The end of the world as we know it requires the work of imagination. The late David Graeber argued that imagination is indispensable in the reproduction of social relations that make our lives meaningful.[1] And, as a friend once told me, *Imagination is movement.* But what if and when movement is denied? How can imagination be a tool of subversion, as countless times feminists have reminded us, if and when imagination is under siege? When the right of mobility is denied, what kind of language and imagination emerge from this place of immobility?

It all started when my colleague, multidisciplinary artist Shuruq Harb, and I began discussing a project, which we provisionally called "living alongside the holy and the cursed."[2] We wanted to give voice to what we felt was the overwhelming feeling of "being stuck"—Shuruq, within the realities of the occupation of Palestine, and myself, within the Italian politics North-South.

Despite the presumed Mediterranean's "liquidity," and the movements happening at sea, our respective regions were living in a state of social paralysis, collapse, and immobility. This immobility is captured in the words of Palestinian scholar Abdaljawad Omar as a situation in which "the past appears tragic, the present perpetual, and the future impossible."[3] The sense of longing for an impossible future and an irretrievable past can become a regressive fantasy. On the other hand, the work of imagination is a way out of this untenable present. As Mahmoud Darwish says to his prison guard, "Dreaming is my profession while yours is pointless eavesdropping on an unfriendly conversation between my freedom and me."[4] For Darwish, poetry is "active freedom." It is the possibility of imagining alternative scenarios outside the present realities of oppression. He uses dreams and memories as forms of resistance, a means to achieve justice. Poetry, he writes, "makes what is visible invisible when facing danger …." In this respect, poetry also asks a question of veracity, of witnessing *the truth* by preserving the imagined, especially in a situation where speaking the truth can cost a life.

In the many conversations with Harb, the question of how to capture the paradox of living with the realities of immobility and alienation caused by the long and violent Israeli occupation is a question of seeking out a language that

DOI: 10.4324/9781003492634-9

Imagination Besieged 81

dignifies and dreams alternative scenarios rather than reproducing violence. A language that can speak without saying, that is, without enacting the oppressive narrative of the occupation.

Through two examples, two works by Palestinian multidisciplinary artist Shuruq Harb and Danish-Palestinian film director Mahdi Fleifel, this essay reflects on different ways in which this sense of melancholy, of "being stuck," is seen from the two different perspectives, viewpoints, and angles of the two shores of the Mediterranean; from the viewpoint of those who stayed and of those who left, both locked, as we shall see, into a deadly dance. In both examples, this sense of alienation and immobility is seen as a symptom of larger processes of structural violence, and at least in the case of Harb's work, paradoxically as an ambiguous form of refusal, a response to the violence of the settler colonial state.

The feeling that the present is "perpetual and the future is impossible" is a condition many youth across the shores of the Mediterranean have become accustomed to: the impossibility of imagining a way out from the scenarios of crisis and destruction that materialise daily in their lives—in the challenges presented by the impossibility of moving; the absence of perspectives; economic and social collapse; environmental and man-made disasters; sense of abandonment; and absence of cultural or educational initiatives. The perpetuity, the reproduction of a present that does not seem to progress, is an exhausting feeling. One that eats away from aspirations and desires. It kills the soul. It produces a general state of debilitation.

"The state wants to exhaust us, they don't want us to be active members of society," Kareem, a Syrian friend who had been a refugee in Greece for more than eight years, tells me. He's referring to the total failure of European migration policies. But he's not necessarily talking about the spectacular facts of border violence and all that we have learnt about Mediterranean border crossing through studies, reportages, and the media. He's talking about a more subtle and insidious form of violence: the physical and mental exhaustion that refugees are forced into by lengthy and dehumanising administrative processes. Refugees are kept in an administrative limbo, in places where they cannot speak the language and are lost in translation; their bodies are contained within the borders of detention centres and camps, and if they receive their "papers," they live with the anxieties that these can be revoked at any time by the hosting country.

This struggle for bare survival makes it much harder for a refugee to exercise their rights and achieve social recognition. Laura Lo Presti has observed that the control, criminalisation, and punishment of movement across the Mediterranean have produced what she described as "immobilization," referring to the "processes of physical, political, mediatic, and aspirational stillness and interruption that migrants are forced to confront when they attempt to move across countries, continents, and seas."[5] If the Mediterranean Sea has been described as a liquid continent,[6] its politics of immobility,

82 *Imagination Besieged*

Lo Presti argues, have effectively "repressed" any idea of historical becoming. People not only remain stuck into an administrative loophole; the continuous violence and stress they're exposed to, alongside traumas they've experienced in their homeland or along the journey, wear out their psychology, deeply affecting their emotional and cognitive abilities.

The loss of intergenerational links, cultural heritage, and a sense of belonging to a place produces a kind of "slow death." My friends not only "feel" stuck but also they are stuck in cycles of dispossession and violence, where the continuous humiliation of checkpoints, controls, and infinite visa processes, the insecurities and uncertainties produced by this state of perennial crisis, the calculated wearing out of life's energies become exhaustion and a deterrent against their dreams and aspirations. Crisis is a common dimension of both sides of the Mediterranean. We're in the same storm. But it is also a system that deeply divides our experiences and sets our realities, those of the "already liberated" and of the unfree, apart.

It is well documented[7] how Israeli regime is inflicting an (attempted) social death upon Palestinians by dispossessing them of their lands and denying their existence, their rights to assemble, to have a home, to cultivate the land, to have a "normal" life. This sense of alienation, the impossibility of conducting a normal life, creates more traumas. Depression is the debilitation of the body and of the soul. Studies have shown that the mental health of Palestinians is among the lowest in the world. They call it the "silent epidemic,"[8] with over half of Palestinian adults living with mental distress, anxiety, and depressive symptoms.[9]

A similar fate attests to the experience of young Syrians, but also Africans, Pakistanis, Bangladeshis, and people from other nationalities who have firsthand encounters with the dehumanising practices of nation-states. A 2015 study by the United Nations Population Fund has found that 41% of Syrian refugee youth living in Lebanon had thought about committing suicide; similarly, in the Gaza Strip, the long siege has produced an increase in mental health problems among the youths. As a group of researchers observed in their research record, "because Palestine is a country with scarce resources from years of humanitarian crisis, it has left its residents with mental scars unseen by the rest of the world."[10] This "unseen" is to be recorded here, precisely because it is also what the settler colonial state does not want it to be recorded and accounted for.

The impossibility to move, to live a normal life, produces a sense of alienation, which eventually leads to resignation, melancholia, depression, suicidal thoughts, and other mental health disorders and disabilities. Because living in a state of constant exception makes one unable to accomplish even the most basic task. In *The Right to Maim: Debility, Capacity, Disability* (2017), Scholar Jasbir Paur speaks of "debility," [11] as a harmful condition perpetuated against a people to biopolitically manage them. Debilitation is one way, Paur argues, to rid of a population who is dehumanised to the point that harm to

Imagination Besieged 83

them is considered "natural." It thus becomes accepted that people who are not white or don't have privileges can die at sea delineated by a bomb or beaten to death; to see them locked up and tortured in overcrowded prisons and camps; that young boys live in fear and with anxieties. And even if some lucky ones make it to this side of the Mediterranean, as my friend K. says, they're effectively disabled in their humanity and in the exercise of their rights.

In her study, Paur shows how some people might not be included in the identity of the disabled body, but in fact, they are. The concept of debility comprehends those bodies that are sustained in a perpetual state of debilitation precisely through foreclosing the social, cultural, and political translation to disability. Because of their marginalisation, these people cannot claim the disabled identity. However, can one call them able-bodied in the same way as someone with other privileges? Puar's answer is no. Using Palestine as an example, she writes, "[a]s the inhabitants of the West Bank are suffering ... no one is constituted as an idealized able body."[12] Most Palestinians endure forms of collective punishment that restrict the mobility for nearly everyone. Puar describes the way the occupation not only uses checkpoints, divided highways, and illegal settlements to fragment the Palestinian's landscape but also targets young people on their knees, creating "infrastructural impediment to deliberately inhibit and prohibit movement."

The study does not focus on the psychological effects of this process of debilitation, but the mental and physical effects of experiences of war and continuous violence of the occupation are the most obvious manifestation of what Puar calls "the right to maim," that is, "the infliction of injury and the maintenance of a perpetually debilitated, but living, Palestinian population under Israeli control."[13]. The everyday obstacles for Palestinians to gain access, move, meet friends and relatives, or simply go to work are so many that eventually people get sick, are forced to live with anxieties, stress, exhausted and debilitated by the deadly grind of the occupation.

How does one call this form of incapacitation that affects imagination? And how does one speak it when the language at our disposal to describe it inflicts more violence, how does one resist it? *The Jump*[14] (2021) a short film by Palestinian multidisciplinary artist Shuruq Harb, interrogates suicide as ultimate and extreme act of ending, of leaping into the void, as both potential thrill, sense of freedom, and definitive end. Prompted by the premature death of a friend and set within the tectonic rift of the Jordan Valley, a deep geological depression, the film is narrated by a robotic voice that guides us through disorienting aerial shots of the landscape. "How can we jump, and what does it mean to jump high?" The voice-over speculating on what it might be like jumping from the high depression of the spectacular Jordan Valley. Its "cold" musing is interrupted by the conversations with two women, literary professor Wafa Darwish and the trauma healer and psychologist Laila Atshan.

In speculating over the suicide of the young man, who jumped into the waters of the Mediterranean Sea, the two women offer important insight into

84 *Imagination Besieged*

the possible meanings and motives of the act of jumping. "Jumping is like an adventure," sitting at the border of the pool one of the two women says. "I understand it. If someone wants to die without fear, jumping is a fun experience ... so one dies happy ... euphoria makes one forget where one is heading to." The other woman adds that jumping into the water is like abandoning the obstacles that the occupation puts on people's everyday lives. The two women reflect on what it means to live with disability and in a state of debilitation, and how they have found ways, small gestures, of healing.

Sitting by the swimming pool, Laila observes that, for an occupied people, it's important to find ways of expression and of being outside the oppressive eye of the occupation. In water, one finds a space where all obstacles, she says, can be removed. Water offers comfort; it's a place where the pain and fear of death can be abandoned for a moment. As the film unravels, so does the meaning and significance of this leap into the void in the context of the occupation; of what it means to "jump" when one is living physically and mentally besieged.

The extreme act of disappearance, of becoming one with the landscape, is mirrored and counteracted by the women's presences, their bodies, and the body of water they use to exercise in the rehabilitation centre. Through its visual language and the montage, the act of jumping is held in tension, as the verb "jumping" remains open to interpretation, between profound despair and total freedom. *The Jump* follows on the path of another short film, *The White Elephant*[15] (2018), which grappled with the effects of the occupation on the psychologies of both the occupied and the occupiers. If the Jump contends with the question of living with death, *The White Elephant* reflects on the consequences of the signing of the Oslo Accord. Oslo was a failure Palestinians paid hard. Using the format of the love letter of a teenager girl to her martyred ex-lover, a car thief, the film is a critical assessment of the fragmented landscape of the occupied territories, and its impact on the lives and mental health of the people.

As Jonathan Lear argues in "Radical Hope," the collapse of a collective way of life that enables populations to thrive cannot be taken lightly: "we necessarily inhabit a way of life that is expressed in a culture. But our way of life—whatever it is—is vulnerable in various ways. And we, as participants in that way of life, thereby inherit a vulnerability. Should that way of life break down, that is our problem."[16] This is precisely what the fragmentation of the territory does; it destroys not only the buildings and material artefacts but also the possibilities of building a sense of community and identity.

The voice-over in the film at a certain moment poses a crucial question: "When you take something apart, how in the world do you remember how it's supposed to go back together?" The disassembling and reassembling of a car becomes a metaphor for an entire community and its territorial dismemberment. Can the irreparable damage be repaired? A dove flies with a white elephant hanging from its beak. In the British dictionary, "A white elephant"

Imagination Besieged 85

is "a possession that is useless or troublesome, especially one that is expensive to maintain or difficult to dispose of." What or who is "the white elephant" if not the Oslo Peace Process? As the artist states, "It literally fragmented the landscape, eroding any Palestinian geographic continuity. It was and still is an expensive corrupt project (I say project rather than peace agreement)." Where there is no sense of "whole" how do you reconstruct a sense of belonging, of identity?

Weaved with the story of a friendship and of the political moment is the simultaneous emergence of the trance music scene in Tel Aviv. Trance music offers young Israeli soldiers a chance to "forget" the war. The protagonist, a young Palestinian girl, manages to disguise herself, smuggle herself into Israel and join the rave. As the voice-over tells, "We all wanted to escape from something, him as a soldier, us to disappear..." It's a powerful and disturbing statement. In conversation, Harb tells me that,

> Actually, Palestinians and Israelis do not come together, because coming together means recognizing one another. The only thing they have in common is that they both are trying to escape from themselves. But that escape means different things to Israelis and to Palestinians. What it means is that for that moment they simply wanted to escape who they are and what it means to be who they are within that context. Since they are trying to disguise themselves, escapism means something else to them in relation to the other Israeli teenage soldiers who are there. They can't simply let go. They can be happy because they are undetected, but they can't be completely free.[17]

This is a crucial point—the fact that despite sharing the same space, the youth do not share the same positionality; they exist in parallel realities— the Israelis are afforded privileges and rights that, on the contrary, are entirely denied to Palestinians. At the same time, paradoxically, the way to disguise this difference is by pretending to be similar. But the truth is, they're not equal, and "escape," "freedom," "mobility," and "disappearance" mean different things because they're experienced differently. Palestinians have to find creative ways of dealing with the restrictions imposed by the occupation. But theirs is not a choice, and it puts them in a position of impossibility because any form of escape is somehow already framed to fail.

Harb's works deal with the distortions produced by the realities of living with the occupation, and the spaces of refusal that open, and through which the protagonists of her stories enact their agency. But if creativity is a form of resistance, it is at the same time being eroded day by day, exhausted as more and more people get sick, die, and are crippled by the occupation. Those who manage to escape this open prison, however, do not always and necessarily find freedom but are exposed to more humiliation, forced into another kind

86 *Imagination Besieged*

of marginality and alienation, that, for instance, of being an asylum seeker in Southern Europe.

There are many film and visual productions in recent years that have documented the alienation experienced by asylum seekers and migrants coming to Europe. *Io Capitano* (2023) by Matteo Garrone, for instance, documents the difficult journey of two Senegalese young men, Seydou and Moussa, to reach Europe. Others, like *Atlantique* (2019) by Mati Diop, through fiction, address the youth malaise, the sense of alienation, and the desire for change experienced by Senegalese youths, and that prompts them to undertake dangerous journeys via sea. In the short documentary *Xenos* (2014) film-director Mahdi Fleifel,[18] captures with disarming depth and simplicity the existential drama lived by many Middle-Eastern refugees and asylum seekers who undertook dangerous journey with the hope of living a better life in Europe.

Instead of finding a refuge, freedom, and better living conditions away from war, violence, despotic regimes, and lunatic dictators, they found themselves stranded in Greece or Southern Italy. In Xenos, a group of Palestinian men from the Ain el-Helweh refugee camp in Lebanon got themselves smuggled through Syria and Turkey and got stuck in Athens. They found themselves stranded in a country, Greece, gripped by economic, political, and social collapse.

There are no jobs, and no opportunities in Southern Europe. And soon enough, the young men realised many Greeks themselves have nothing to put on their table. One of the most moving lines in *Xenos* is when Abu Eyad steals a Greek woman's purse in Athens, discovers it only has seven euros, and says, "I found that she was starving too." The 13-minute-long short film documentary, shot in the streets of Athens during the difficult years of the economic crisis, is accompanied by the voice-over of a telephone conversation between the film-maker himself and Abu Eyad, in which one man updates the other on their situation: his friends started taking drugs, and when not on drugs, they get depressed and aggressive, while he sometimes prostitutes himself in the park to buy cigarette and some food. While their families in Lebanon think that they're looking for jobs, the reality is that they struggle to survive. They live in a limbo, in a country hostile to foreigners and broken by an economic and social decline. When asked about his "job in the park," Abu Eyad describes the dilemma he finds himself in, stealing or prostituting. Annoyed by the friend's insistence, he says, "I need to survive. What else am I going to do?"

Fleifel's short documentary captures the human drama suffered by Palestinians and other migrants in those places of transition. "This country ruins your soul," is Abu Eyad's bitter and desperate conclusion. This last line describes so succinctly and with arrow-like precision the kind of suffering and degradation that those young men experience.[19] Fleifel's film does not tell an exemplary story with happy endings, or a tragic one, that could raise the sympathies of the audience. Xenos, I believe, doesn't look for the audience's

Imagination Besieged 87

empathy like many films on migration tend to do. It tells realistically of the everyday struggle of those who, trying to escape suffering in one place, losing their familial ties, found themselves among the ruins of the European project of modernisation. All they want is to have a better life and, like us, says the film-maker, "they have dreams and fears and hopes. But they're stuck."[20]

It is the debilitation and degradation of human life that happens not only in the camps and shelters but very much also in the streets, the abandoned buildings, and the dark alleys of Athens. Here, the so-called "refugee crisis" meets the consequences of Greece's economic crisis producing an explosive environment. Many make use of drugs to survive the daily struggle, and many begin to struggle with drug addiction. To attribute this to personal weaknesses would be a dangerous mistake because it would be to deny the materialities of structural violence in the mental health and well-being of people.

Both Harb and Fleifel's short films speak to the affective and psychological consequences of living under "siege"—physically, psychologically, metaphorically, politically, socially, and economically. And be under siege twice: once in the places they have escaped from, and again in the places they arrived to. In both cases, the protagonists live in an extreme situation of dehumanisation and marginalisation which has become their "normality." Abandoned by a social system that is incapable of protecting them, and instead criminalises them, they're pushed to the edge and try to find freedom in whatever way they can, within the perimeter of freedom afforded to them. How to blame them for their desire to escape?

Differences notwithstanding, both Harb and Fleifel's films ask a fundamental question, about attending to the deep implications that living under this perennial state of siege can have on the ability to have and pursue aspirations, desires, and imagine alternatives. If Harb uses fiction, archival images, and poetry to give voice to those questions, Fleifel's documentary approach offers a straightforward, realistic portrait of the refugee's experience.

Their works represent two different and complementary ways of bearing witness to this moment of "escape" from an impossible situation of imprisonment. A paradoxical position which is both symptomatic of the realities of alienation experienced by the protagonists of their stories. The protagonists are escaping something. But their escape is often one that they have not chosen and on which they have limited agency. They live in a precarious and ambiguous situation, and they live "freedom" in a deeply ambiguous manner.

Notes

1 David Graeber, "Value as the importance of action", in La balsa de piedra, n 6, enero-marzo 2014. Available through: https://davidgraeber.org/articles/value-as-the-importance-of-actions/

2 See also, https://www.onassis.org/initiatives/onassis-air/onassis-air-programs-2022-23/federica-bueti-living-alongside-the-holy-and-the-cursed

88 *Imagination Besieged*

3 Omar Abdaljawad, "Can the Palestinians Mourn?," in rustedradishes online, 2024.
4 Mahmoud Darwish, *In the Presence of Absence*, p. 4.
5 Available through: https://www.e-flux.com/journal/109/330800/like-a-map-over-troubled-water-un-mapping-the-mediterranean-sea-s-terraqueous-necropolitics/
6 Nicholas Purcell, *The Liquid Continent: A Study of Mediterranean History* (Blackwell Pub., 2010).
7 Haddad, M. (2022) "Nakba Day: What Happened in Palestine in 1948?," *Al Jazeera* 15 May. Available through: https://www.aljazeera.com/news/2022/5/15/nakba-mapping-palestinian-villages-destroyed-by-israel-in-1948 (Accessed: 7 January 2024).

Holman, Z. (2023) "Palestine: From Accord to Apartheid," *The New Internationalist.* Available through: https://newint.org/features/2023/06/05/big-story-palestine-accord-apartheid-occupation-israel#:~:text=A%20new%20far%2Dright%20Israeli,are%20still%20off%20the%20table (Accessed: 8 January 2024).

Ingalla, S. (2023) "The Profit Behind Israel's Apartheid of Palestine," *Philippine Collegian.* Available through: https://phkule.org/article/1024/the-profit-behind-israels-apartheid-of-palestine (Accessed: 8 January 2024).

Khalidi, R. *The Hundred Years' War on Palestine: A History of Settler Colonialism and Resistance, 1917–2017* (Metropolitan Books, 2020).

Malik, N. (2023) "What does it mean to erase a people—a nation, culture, identity? In Gaza, we are beginning to find out," *The Guardian*, 18 December. Available through: https://www.theguardian.com/commentisfree/2023/dec/18/gaza-israel-destroying-culture-and-identity (Accessed: 7 January 2024).

Masalha, N. *The Palestine Nakba: Decolonising History, Narrating the Subaltern, Reclaiming Memory* (Bloomsbury Publishing, 2012).

Pappé, I. "The 1948 Ethnic Cleansing of Palestine," *Journal of Palestine Studies*, *36*(1), 6–20, 2006. doi:10.1525/jps.2006.36.1.6.

Pappé, I. (2014) "Israel's incremental genocide in the Gaza ghetto," *The Electronic Intifada.* Available through: https://electronicintifada.net/content/israels-incremental-genocide-gaza-ghetto/13562 (Accessed: 8 January 2024).

Said, E.W., *The Question of Palestine* (New York, NY: Vintage Books, 1992).

United Nations. UN General Assembly (1948). *Convention on the Prevention and Punishment of the Crime of Genocide* (9 December 1948). United Nations, Treaty Series, vol. 78, p. 277. Available through: https://www.refworld.org/legal/agreements/unga/1948/en/13495 (Accessed: 5 January 2024).

Wise, L.E. "Social Death and the Loss of a 'World': An Anatomy of Genocidal Harm in Sudan," *The International Journal of Human Rights, 21*(7), 838–865, 2017. doi:10.1080/13642987.2017.1310464.

8 Shukri, Said; Holmes, David; Shukri, Nabeel; Shukri, Hassan; and Saada, Fahed (2023) "The silent epidemic; the toll of mental health in occupied Palestine," *Palestinian Medical and Pharmaceutical Journal*: Vol. 8 : Iss. 1 , Article 5. Available through: https://pmpj.najah.edu/cgi/viewcontent.cgi?article=1141&context=journal
9 Source: Available through: https://www.nature.com/articles/s41598-023-43293-6
10 Bdier, D., Veronese, G. & Mahamid, F. Quality of life and mental health outcomes: the role of sociodemographic factors in the Palestinian context. *Sci Rep* 13, 16422 (2023). Available through: https://pmpj.najah.edu/cgi/viewcontent.cgi?article=1141&context=journal

Imagination Besieged 89

11 Puar states that "[d]ebility addresses injury and bodily exclusion that are endemic rather than epidemic or exceptional." Puar, *The Right to Maim*, xvii.
12 Puar, *The Right to Maim*, 158.
13 Puar, *The Right to Maim*, X.
14 Shuruq Harb, *The Jump* (2020), one-channel video, 10 mins.
15 Shuruq Harb, *The White Elephant* (2018), one-channel video, 12 mins.
16 Jonathan Lear, *Radical Hope: Ethics in the Face of Cultural Devastation* (Harvard University Press, 2007). See also review. Available through: https://normalenews.sns.it/radical-hope-ethics-in-the-face-of-cultural-devastation#:~:text=Lear%20writes%3A,with%20which%20to%20understand%20it
17 From a conversation with the artist on the occasion of the exhibition "Ecologies of Darkness" at SAVVY Contemporary, Berlin, January 2019. Unpublished.
18 Mahdi Fleifel, *Xenos* (2013), 13 mins.
19 Even though more than ten years have passed, the situation has not changed. In a conversation I had with two young Iraqi of 20 and 21 years old, they lamented the dehumanising conditions in which they're forced to still live and work and the general poor social and economic condition of the country, which pushed many of them to try to find ways to reach the more prosperous North.
20 Alex Ritman, "Mahdi Fleifel on His Scorsese-Inspired Palestinian Refugee Thriller to a Land Unknown," in Variety, July 2024. Available through: https://variety.com/2024/film/global/mahdi-fleifel-to-a-land-unknown-galway-1236067602/

9 Movements at Sea[1]

(Annotations on "Off You Shore Paper Trail"[2])

When we began working on our collaboration, Shuruq and I knew that, in order to speak of our "shared home," we wanted to take the way of the sea, of that Mediterranean that was both barrier and point of connection between shores and people. A place of mobility, invoking liquid imaginaries of journeying, crossing, nomadism, transformation, exchanges, and contaminations. Yet, despite the liquidity of the sea[3] our respective regions, as we have observed over the years, are frozen: Calabria is stuck within Italian's inequities that divide the rich North from the poor and infrastructurally crippled South.[4] Palestine is a more complex and highly volatile environment. The jurisdiction of the land is being contested in a way that makes it difficult for Palestinian artists to freely move, live, and work without constantly having to explain or justify their existence and practices.

In this chapter, I attempt to piece together and trace the route of the journey which led to the making of a short experimental film, *Off You Shore Paper Trail*, 2024. The film asks questions about migration, trade, security interests, movement, and accessibility. The film addresses one of the central questions of this book, which is the kind of imagination that this feeling of "being stuck" produces, and the kind of language it demands not only to grapple with its realities but to imagine to overcome it.

How could we express this "shared" feeling, this sense of "home," without losing the differences, the dissonances, and the contradictions? How could we find a language that would disclose but also protect the imagined at the heart of this sense of "stuckness"? Eduard Glissant's poetic of relation offers a poetic way to deal with the obfuscations and oppressive language and discourse of the coloniser by way of what he calls "diversion." He explains that diversion is a way of looking for one's own roots in another place than "home." Since colonial history is obfuscated and rendered invisible in the very act of being imposed in order to portray the colonial situation as necessary, the source of oppression is not immediately clear to the consciousness of the oppressed. To find the source of oppression, then it is necessary to adopt an approach that Glissant calls "parallactic"—moving and changing the position in order to see an objective that was previously covered by an obstacle.

DOI: 10.4324/9781003492634-10

The condition for the success of this parallactic strategy, as a means to survive, depends on the possibility of finding concrete obstacles that the detour can elude by shifting positions. In *Caribbean Discourse*, Glissant specifically identifies the multiplicity and hybridity of Creole as a *rhizomatic strategy of diversion* that provides the occasion for countering the idea of "root." In the face of the colonisers' attempt to fix and silence the enslaved as mute and empty, Glissant proposes Creole as a "systematic process of derision." "You wish to reduce me to a childish babble, I will make this babble systematic, we shall see if you can make sense of it."[5] Creole, for instance—its hybridity, multiplicity, ambiguity, improperness and the disorder it creates– becomes a counter-hegemonic language; one that problematizes the idea of "origin" and invents its own form. However, for Glissant, it's important that this detour does not lose sight of the fact that the ultimate goal is always to (re)construct a liberated condition.

The way we approached the subject of our research was indeed by way of diversions, by looking for "home" in unexpected places and at a distance from both our respective realities, we were trying not only to see the kind of invisible threads that run through and link different manifestation of systems of oppression but very much also to release ourselves from it and to find a language and strategies to deceive its grip on imagination. We approached our different realities by making a detour through what we considered a sort of "middle point"; a place both familiar and unknown; a city where we felt both at home ad foreign; a location different from our respective "homes", but where we could explore shared legacies, certain "problems" were made more visible.

In a sense, it was not by chance that Athens and the histories of Greek maritime shipping became central to our research. After all, looking at global shipping from this location made it possible to visualise more clearly the histories and links between the emergenceof global shipping after WWII and the larger geopolitical tecctonic shifts. Shipping is the place where the histories of post-war Europe, decolonisation, the Nation-State, and its nationalist discourse intersect. To think with shipping about the post-war process of modernisation, the occupation of Historic Palestine, and the deep transformation brought about decolonisation and financialisation offers a possibility to address questions about Palestine and Calabria through this interdependent and entangled perspective.

In 2022, when we finally had the opportunity to be physically in Athens[6]. Our research started taking shape as we walked through the hills of Philopappos and Lycabettus, the ruins of the Acropolis, down towards the sea. Through long walks, we did some environmental sound and video recordings. We walked to Pireaus and its harbour, where we spent hours observing the maritime traffic—the big cargo, the tankers, the small cargo, the passenger, tourist, and military ships docking and leaving the big port in an incessant loading and unloading, coming and going.

Looking west, looking east by northeast, looking northwest, looking northeast, looking south, looking north, looking east, looking west, looking north,

92 *Imagination Besieged*

looking northeast, old ships. The sea became our means of transportation, the site of imagination. But, while we were looking at the same sea, we were not really looking at the same thing. The sea spoke differently to our different experiences: I was born in a small village of fishermen, and the sea had been in my life since I was a child; Shuruq, on the other hand, as Palestinian living in the West Bank, had no direct access to the sea,[7] which she could only see from far away. As Suja Sawafta recalls in her memories of childhood,

> The engineering it took to visit and to experience an element of this earth that has formed, if not defined, my genetic memory made the moment I reached the Mediterranean's Egyptian shores all the more significant. And yet, as I reached the edge of the water, a paralysis took hold of me. I was unable to submerge my body into the sea. I thought again of Darwish. I wanted the first time I experienced and fully came to know the Mediterranean to be in my country. I didn't know if the day would ever come; I knew that it might not come. But I also knew, on a cellular level, that I had to wait—and to wait for a Jaffa, specifically.[8]

In this passage, it is expressed all the ambivalence in the experience of the narrator's first encounter with the sea. The joy of the moment, almost immediately interrupted by the realities of the occupation, that are impressed in her body and memory, and that create a strange paralysis—a sense of longing for an absence, a dream of being able to enjoy the sea in her own country. What the narrator feels thus is not really joy, but neither is just sadness. It is something more complex. Something that demands a language and an aesthetic of "listening to" that knows how to pay attention to the silences, the ambiguities and distortions in how we experience realities. I keep walking next to Shuruq, following her steps.

Our walks and observations of the environment were punctuated by meetings and important encounters, such as the one with maritime historian Gelina Harlaftis and the team she was leading in the reconstruction of the Onassis Maritime archive. In our Zoom conversation, Harlaftis highlighted the importance of maritime studies[9] to a history of the relationships and exchanges that shaped the world as we know it today and pointed to the difficulties in creating an archive of those relationships that, for instance, defined the history of Greek maritime power and in fact gave the scale of Greece's contribution to the world economy.[10] With their ships, seafarers, and amazing knowledge and competence, seafarers and shipowners helped the development of the world economy, among others, by solving problems of logistics. At the same time, shipping allowed Greek shipowners to accumulate large profits and, through the system of flags of convenience, they could avoid paying taxes to the Greek government. It can be claimed that those shipowners "gave back" to their beloved country in many other forms. Investment in the cultural sector, including archiving, preservation, restoration, and even support for contemporary

Movements at Sea 93

art museums and institutions in Greece, is very much sponsored by shipowner families such as Onassis. A friend suggested that we go visit the Liberty ship, a "floating museum"[11] and wreck from WWII docked at the port of Piraeus.

Shipwrecks are maps—and they disclose the trade routes, the conflicts, the movements of things and people and are traces and remnants of slow violence that took on and goes deep down the surface of the sea.[12]

The rusty metal sign outside said, "Hellas Liberty Museum." The area of the museum is a passage point for tracks transporting goods going to the Greek islands; the structure where the ship is docked, an old shipyard and repair workshop, is itself a ruin of an industrial time long gone. Access to the floating museum is through the old mobile stairs that dangle dangerously in the void. Once inside, it all looks new. We went back several times, and each time we spent many hours inside the belly of the ship, among empty chairs of what has been turned into a conference room. There were maritime paraphernalia in other rooms and collages of archive images of the various Liberty ships and their respective owners and families. The captions read:

Liberty …: broken in two and declared a total loss.
Liberty …: Collided with a cargo ship, abandoned by its crew and declared a constructive total loss.
Liberty… broken, refloated, declared a total loss, broken up into pieces.
Liberty … broken in three parts and sank outside the port of Beirut. A total constructive loss
Liberty … Hellenic Star. Registered in Piraeus. Transferred to Hellenic lines, Sold to Pleiades Shipping, renamed Aghios Nicolaos and placed under Cypriot flag. Broken up in Istanbul.
Liberty … Ran aground in heavy weather on a reef near Burma and sunk.
Liberty… Ran aground on Isola delle Correnti while on a voyage to Karachi.[13]

The succinct information is written in what sounds like a coded language made of "losses" and "breakages," "transfers," and "indomable-she-ships."[14] A language only the initiated, researchers, and passionate lovers of maritime histories could clearly read, but mostly inaccessible to the uninitiated audience. As we progressed with our research, however, the meaning of those "losses" became clearer. The Liberty was a class of cargo ships built in the USA during WWII. Designed with the idea of an inexpensive and quick production to address the critical needs for transportation, these ships played a crucial role in transporting troops, food, fuel, and military equipment across the Atlantic.[15]

The Liberty was neither a fast nor an innovative ship design-wise. It was rather built following the necessity of a fast replacement of vessels. The only innovation, the extensive use of welding, which offered a quicker construction

94   *Imagination Besieged*

method, was however also its problem, and this explains why many of them sunk, ran aground, or broke into two. When the war was over and the need for Liberty decreased, the American government decided to sell the remaining vessels to other countries.

Having lost more than two-thirds of their fleet during WWII, the Greeks were among the first to purchase Liberty ships. On April 9, 1946, the Greek government guaranteed the purchase of 100 Liberties on behalf of its shipowners, their only obligation being to hoist the Greek flag. In October 1945, Manolis Kouloukountis, a shipowner with great prestige in shipbuilding circles, wrote, "We rely on the Liberty type as the main source of replacement for the sunken Greek ships."[16] The purchase of the Liberty with the help of the Greek government led to a series of controversies and the publication of an article that Onassis wrote about the relationship between state and shipowners, known as "J'e accuse."[17]

Onassis writes, "Family capital, two wars, and the leniency of the state have played a crucial role in accumulation of capital and profits for ethnomartyrs and all the Christopher Columbus of Heaven flags. So, miraculously, the poor turn aristocrats overnight, the pond is transformed into an alabaster swimming pool in Crete, the goats of the island into Pekinois butlers from Paris. We have to admit that if Dostoyevsky were alive, he would certainly kill himself out of frustration towards this imagination."[18] His sarcasm was a direct response to the way he felt he had been ostracised by other Greek shipowners. He wanted to enter the Greek shipping "family," but as someone coming from a different business background, as his parents were dealing in tobacco, he felt he was denied his belonging.

In another passage of the article, he writes, "Am I not one of you?" He writes, "Why levantine, why Argentinian? Have I not tried to keep things in the family? So, why rejecting my plans? Why exclude me? According to the rules of geographical citizenship, you were Ottomans, then Italians and months ago Greek."[19] His rhetoric made the Greek shipping aristocracy shiver. He casted himself as a self-made rebel but also a patriot who had not been helped by guarantees from the Greek state.[20]

In his article, Onassis writes that the Greek shipowners didn't need the intervention of the state in the purchase of the vessels since they could make enough profit through insurances and flags of convenience. Why would they want to hoist the Greek flag? Nationalistic reasons didn't make much sense. "What crazy person would invest dollars in a Greek flag?[21] Nevertheless, the purchase of the Liberty ship was important in reinvigorating Greece's collapsed shipping power, and it symbolises, as the association running the museum calls it, "the renaissance of Greek shipping."[22]

As Harlaftis has argued, Shipwrecks are maps—and they disclose the trade routes, the conflicts, the movements of things and people, and the exchanges that took place on the surface of the sea.[23] The Liberty ship Museum is the wreck that keeps the memories and ghosts of twentieth-century nationalist

Movements at Sea 95

discourse alive, while at the same time also recording the transnational movements that took place: the end of WWII, the establishment of the State of Israel, the process of decolonisation, the emergence of transnational forms of "cooperation."

The "weak" nationalism that somehow the Liberty engenders—"weak" because it could not compete with the emergent global economic interests—didn't really work, especially for someone like Onassis 'ambitions and transnational approach to what he rightfully understood as a global affair. He is credited with inventing a new model of raising finances based on loans being paid off by secured long-term charters from reputable oil companies. He effectively used the model of the offshore to sustain and expand his global shipping business operations. In a sense, the Liberty was not only a map of post-war Europe and its re-emergence after the collapse caused by WWII and the civil war. Through Onassis' letter and his link to the purchase of the ships, it also became the map of histories of offshore growth during the post-war and post-colonial period in a way that explains the present. As Onassis understood the enormous economic potential of this economic and financial model, others too, in the European colonies, understood the profitable potential of offshore in moving assets from one collapsing system, that of the colonies, to lands of opportunities, or so-called "tax heaven."

> "Some had read the advertisement in newspapers praising the advantages of bank secret numbered accounts in foreign banks, others had received recruitment letters as potential client, with invitation to open bank accounts in tax heavens."

> "I have some accumulated income earned in West Africa. The funds are now in the Channel Islands. I want to invest this money and will appreciate your advice as to whether such investment can be made in U.K. domiciled companies without the Inland Revenue claiming that such investment constitutes a bringing home of funds."

> "After securing an annual depreciation, within ten years it is possible to foresee an annual surplus of about three hundred thousand dollars for ten years. This amount ensures important and stable profits."[24]

In the late 1960s, as historian Vanessa Ogle observes, "the *Financial Times* and the industry publication the *Banker* began running regular multi-page spreads and special sections detailing the latest developments in offshore destinations, often blurring the line between reporting and free advertising for the tax-avoidance industry."[25] Banks and financial institutions created literally a promotional campaign to educate and encourage settlers to invest capital previously invested in the colonies. Essentially, the settlers' problem was to transfer money and reinvest it avoiding national taxation. It was a way

96 *Imagination Besieged*

to evade what for many businessmen was an unnecessary burden, the State, which hindered their economic progress. What course of action did smaller and less well-known companies and businesses pursue once it was clear that the days of white rule were numbered? Where did this money go? Ogle asks.

If decolonisation brings up memories of political resistance and the movements for liberation, in her study, Ogle has referred to "decolonization" as an "economic and financial event"[26] and argued that alongside this more visible manifestation of the end of colonialism, decolonisation took on the shape of a financial event. The white settlers were trying to "free" capital and move their assets to more stable, safe, and especially tax-free locations. As Ogle writes,

> Many Europeans in the colonial world, especially those who owned land, farms, factories and other enterprises, began fretting about what the end of white rule would mean for their business interests and personal wealth. After decades of coercive and violent European conquest and colonialism, European elites feared that vengeful new leaders might impose taxes and restrictions on their business activity, investments and capital movements after independence.[27]

Decolonisation created a money panic among white settlers. While some money returned to European metropolitan centres, a significant share was moved to the emerging offshore tax havens with their relaxed regulations and minimal taxes; flags of convenience registries; offshore financial markets and banking institutions, which offer investors advantages absent in national financial markets. "This archipelago-like landscape allowed free-market capitalism to flourish on the sidelines of a world dominated by nationalisms."[28] This movement of assets and investments in securities was part, as Ogle observes, of a gradual transformation of the global economy, alongside the state's attempt to emerge as a strong national actor.[29]

However, by artificially reducing earnings in low-income countries, such companies thus deprived newly independent economies of much-needed tax revenue. The implications of such decisions can be imagined, with national economies becoming more reliant on the private sector and dependent on foreign aids and other forms of neo-colonialism. An important point in Ogle's study is that the offshore world contributed to the eventual demise of the mid-century state-based order. "States found that the offshore leakages they had tolerated or actively created were increasingly difficult to contain."[30]

In this way, for Ogle, the "archipelago" of tax havens, offshore financial centres, and foreign trade zones reveals the unfinished project of "the state-based aspirations of the long mid-century, from the New Deal to the redistributive welfare state to the state-driven top-down modernisation politics in the developing world."[31] Instead, offshore has acted like a kind of piracy, stealing not only the resources but also the aspirations and national fantasies. Ogle's insights into the histories of the relationship between offshore and

Movements at Sea 97

decolonisation, and her practice of working with archives, offered us a way to grapple with questions of truths, the veracity of an account, witnessing; with language, with what is considered "legal" and what is defined as "illegal." Wasn't offshore, the way it is described, a legalised form of piracy? Weren't the settlers, after all, searching for convenient and profitable investments, practicing a form of piracy[32]?

If the rules of the game are, as Onassis writes in 1947, already in plain sight, the interesting and paradoxical fact is that up until today many archives of shipping companies remain inaccessible to researchers and the public. As we have experienced and observed during the period of our research, access to private maritime archives is often challenging, if not impossible. And even when access is being granted, the information are carefully selected and curated to emphasise the "achievements." It took us several phone calls and conversations to be granted access to the Liberty for the shooting. And it was even harder to visit private maritime archives of Greek ship-owners. It seemed a bit suspect that two young women would want to pursue such an interest and have so many strange questions. As a shipowner who gently agreed to meet me said, "you're both are strong and fearless women to ask all those questions." Then he laughed. But it remains unclear what he meant, nor did he really share, if not in glimpses, insights into the "secrets" of this global business of logistics without which, as he himself says, we could not live our lives as we do.

Liberty as a shipwreck tells also of this secrecy, and the attempt by power to obfuscate its system that perpetuates inequalities and oppression. Then, there was us inside the ship, trying to capture the hesitancy that many interviewees had shown and how "secrecy" was mirrored in the general atmosphere of the place. Going down the stairs, inside the ship's belly, it became darker and darker, and in the empty space full of empty chairs, the dark light illuminated the shadows. Shadows that got on our way at times, as for instance, when trying to film the captions accompanying the photographs. We try to record the absences and the ghostly presences.

We also wanted to express the ambiguous and slippery nature of the subject—the ambivalence we felt towards many of the events and the protagonists of these stories, who were indeed ambiguous and highly problematic characters; but also the ambiguity of our different experiences of the place, the people, the sea, the movement of the cargo ships, and the freedom of mobility.

We wanted to capture the atmosphere of secrecy and obscurity in which all of these things happen, attempt at erasing and obfuscating the evidence. We were interested in the "intractability" of the information, and in the ways in which we could turn toward this intractable core, and offer a voice to those silences and gaps in the story. We gave voice to them through the form of a dialogue. A dialogue between two researchers, Fede and Shuruq, who are following a paper trail, leading to a series of encounters and discoveries. The dialogue, an exchange of voice-notes, "listens to" and traces the difficulties

98 *Imagination Besieged*

and obstacles two researchers found on their way to find the truth about the links that connect the colonial past to the present of dispossession.

And to go around the obstacle, they had to make a detour; and the detour became the film, going offshore, off-centre, off the beaten trail. "What is it that we're not supposed to know?" Shuruq asks. Darkness and the echoes of our step on the cold metal floor guided us, until we were on the main deck, in the brightness of the daylight, observing the movements, the scale of things around us; the ships going in and out of the port, imagining points of departures and arrivals. Hoping to get on to the other side before sunset to see how the liberty looked from a distance, a perspective that was, surprisingly, completely new. Staring at this relict, small and rusty, in the fresh air of the night, it looked a bit awkward and goofy, also creepy, and at moments disquieting. Its wrecked appearance on the horizon did not intimidate us. The ship looked so small compared to the new ones all around. We were looking at the corpse of modernity, and of a failed process of modernisation; the ruin of an age coming to its end. The Floating Museum will soon be moved to another location, a little tourist harbour, where this relict will find its final resting place. And giggling, we thought between ourselves that, despite the many odds and obstacles, we got to tell our version of the story, as a reminder that defeat is not inevitable.

What can he do to end the process of self-criticism, other than apologize for an existence which has not yet come into being? You are not going there, and you don't belong here. Between these two negations this generation was born defending the spirit's bodily vessel, onto which they fasten the fragrance of the country they've never known. They've read what they've read, and they've seen what they've seen, and they don't believe defeat is inevitable. So they set out on the trail of that fragrance.[33]

Notes

1 This text documents part of the process of making Off You Paper Trail and reflects some of the important conversations I had with artist and collaborator Shuruq Harb throughout the period of research and making of the film. In this sense, this text is written in dialogue with Harb, who is and has been an invaluable and inspiring collaborator. This text is dedicated to her.

2 "Off You Paper Trail,"10 mins, (2024), is a collaboration with artist Shuruq Harb and a short-film commissioned by the Busan Biennale Committee, 2024.

Following the eerie demise of these ships, which often undertook tragically fated journeys, the film comes to terms with inherent contradictions of archiving offshore finance documents. Filming into and around the liberty ship, which became a catalyst for the complex relation to the Mediterranean basin shared by both authors, allowed for musings about imaginations of sharing, movement, and accessibility, in contrast with a reality of police control, interruption, or being stuck without the possibility of leaving. The Liberty ship carries memories of hope and despair relating to narratives of return and becomes a haunting vessel for ruminations about migration, tourism, trade, and security interests. Following the eerie demise of these ships, which often undertook tragically fated journeys, the film comes to terms with the inherent contradictions of archiving and what resists such preservation, to engage with the unspoken, unrecorded histories and subversive ways of movement of people and goods. More info: https://busanbiennale2024.com/en/exhibition/artists/08641861-7aab-40f7-a0b2-d28a62cf0193

3 Peregrine Horden and Nicholas Purcell, *The Corrupting Sea: A Study of Mediterranean History* (WILEY Blackwell, 2020).

4 Luizabcl, "The North-South Divide and Its Long-Lasting Effects on Italian Culture," Nuitalian.org, April 27, 2023. Domenico Cersosimo e Sabina Licurdi, *Lento Pede. Vivere nell'Italia estrema* (Donizelli, 2023).

5 Glissant, *Caribbean Discourse*, p. 20.

6 We were hosted at and the research was partly supported by Onassis AiR— Residency Program, in February and March 2022. Available through: https://www.onassis.org/initiatives/onassis-air/onassis-air-programs-2022-23/federica-bueti-living-alongside-the-holy-and-the-cursed

7 Suja Sawafta, Two Shores, One Sea. Login for Palestine's Mediterranean, February 28, 2024.
The Buffler, February 2024. Available through: https://thebaffler.com/latest/two-shores-one-sea-sawafta; Nikos Kosmatopoulos, "A People's Sea: Palestine and Popular Thalassopolitics in the Mediterranean Sea," *Millennium, 51*(3), 739–757, 2023.

8 Suja Sawafta, Two Shores, One Sea. Login for Palestine's Mediterranean, February 28, 2024.
The Buffler, February 2024. Available through: https://thebaffler.com/latest/two-shores-one-sea-sawafta

9 See Gelina Harlaftis, "Maritime History: A New Version of the Old Version and the True History of the Sea," *The International Journal of Maritime History, 32*(2), 383–402, 2020.

10 See Gelina Harlaftis, "The Onassis Global Shipping Business, 1920s–1950s," *Business History Review, 88*(Summer), 241–271, 2014.

11 Available through: https://www.hellaslibertymuseum.gr/en/

12 This excerpt from the script for the first draft of Off You Paper Trail, 2020.

13 These are snippets from the captions accompanying the archival photographs shown inside the Liberty Hellas Museum. They are included in the script for the voice-over of the film.

14 Interestingly, we noticed that all captions used "she" to refer to the ships. Sometime later, I found a poster at the office of a shipowner, which explains the use of the "she" in this way, "A ship is called a 'she' because there is always a great deal of bustle around her, there is usually a gang of men around; she has a waist and stays; it takes a lot of paint to keep her good looking; it is not the initial expense that breaks you, it is the upkeep; she can be all decked out; it takes an experienced man to handle her; and without a man at the helm, she is absolutely uncontrollable. She shows her top-sides, hides her bottom, and when coming into part, always heads for the buoys." Syros Island, July, 2024.

15 Available through: https://navalhistoria.com/the-liberty-ships-of-world-war-ii-an-icon-of-american-industrial-might/#Origins-Of-The-Liberty-Ships

16 Gelina Harlaftis, Τζελίνα Χαρλαύτη, Το "κατηγορώ" του Αριστοτέλη Ωνάση προς τους εφοπλιστές και την ελληνική κυβέρνηση το 1947, Ιόνιος Λόγος, 2013. All translation from this text, unless specified, are mine.

17 Ibid.

18 Ibid.

19 Ibid.

100 *Imagination Besieged*

20 Available through: https://greekshippinghalloffame.org/?inductee=aonassis-en

21 Let me explain to you that this is *a card game*, he says. Picture this. A ship worth 20,000 pounds, ten of which are covered by debt. War is declared, and we insure it, paying a premium of about 10,000 pounds for a 60-day trip. If the voyage ends and the ship arrives, it leaves us with a loss of many thousands of pounds. Now, as we already owed £10,000 out of the twenty thousand the ship is worth, if the war were to stop suddenly, the bankruptcy would be instantaneous. On the contrary, if the ship was torpedoed, it makes a fabulous profit, not to say a fortune. So, what is next to wish for? Of course, the catastrophic, the shipwreck, if possible, without loss of souls (!)(...)" in Gelina Harlaftis, Τζελίνα Χαρλαύτη, Το "κατηγορώ" του Αριστοτέλη Ωνάση προς τους εφοπλιστές και την ελληνική κυβέρνηση το 1947, Ιόνιος Λόγος, 2013.

22 Available through: https://www.hellaslibertymuseum.gr/en/the-museum/

23 This excerpt from the script for the first draft of Off You Paper Trail, 2020.

24 The three quotes are all from Vanessa Ogle, "FUNK MONEY: The End of Empire, The Expansion of Tax-Havens, and Decolonization as Economic and Financial Event" in Past and Present, no. 249 (Nov. 2020).

25 Vanessa Ogle, "The end of empire and the rise of tax havens. How decolonisation propelled the growth of low-tax jurisdictions, with lasting economic implications for former colonies" in The New Statesman, December 2020. Available through: https://www.newstatesman.com/ideas/2020/12/end-empire-and-rise-tax-havens

26 See Vanessa Ogle, "Archipelago Capitalism: Tax Havens, Offshore Money, and the State, 1950s–1970s," *American Historical Review*, *122*(5), 1431–1458, December 2017.

27 Vanessa Ogle, "The end of empire and the rise of tax havens. How decolonisation propelled the growth of low-tax jurisdictions, with lasting economic implications for former colonies," in The New Statesman, December 2020. Available through: https://www.newstatesman.com/ideas/2020/12/end-empire-and-rise-tax-havens

28 Vanessa Ogle, "Archipelago Capitalism: Tax Havens, Offshore Money, and the State, 1950s–1970s," *American Historical Review*, *122*(5), 1431–1458, December 2017.

29 Vanessa Ogle, "FUNK MONEY: The End of Empire: The Expansion of Tax-Havens, and Decolonization as Economic and Financial Event," in Past and Present, no. 249 (Nov. 2020).

30 Ogle, Archipelago Capitalism, 1457.

31 Ogle, Archipelago Capitalism, 1457.

32 Professor Nabil Matar, who has written extensively trying to offer a more balanced view of the Mediterranean in early modern times, observes that the perceived threat of Barbary pirates was not realistic and in fact, expressed an overtly anti-Muslim narrative. "By 1830 the fleets of Europe were by far more powerful, more sophisticated, more advanced in their military technology than North Africans; it was an excuse for colonisation rather than eradication of piracy," he writes. Nabil Matar, *Mediterranean Captivity through Arab Eyes* (Brill, 2021).

33 Mahmood Darwish, *Memory for Forgetfulness*, translated and with an intro. by Ibrahim Muhawi, and with a new foreword by Sinan Antoon (University of California Press, 1995), 17.

Bibliography

Omar Abdaljawad, "Can the Palestinians Mourn?", *Rusted Radishes—Beirut Literary and Art Journal*, 2024.

David Abulafia, *The Great Sea. A Human History of the Mediterranean* (Allen Lane edition, 2011).

Etel Adnan, *Sitt Marie Rose*, translated by Georgina Kleege (Sausalito, CA: Post-Apollo Press, 1982). Sara Ahmed, "Dated Feminists", blog, 2014.

Sara Ahmed, "Feminist Attachment", in *The Cultural Politics of Emotion* (Edinburgh: Edinburgh University Press, 2014).

Sara Ahmed, "Feminist Killjoys (And Other Willful Subjects)", in *Poliphonic Feminisms. Acting in Concert, S&F* Online, Issue 8, Summeer 2010.

Sara Ahmed, "It's not the time for a party", blog, 2015.

Sara Ahmed, "Nodding as a non-performative", blog, 2019.

Corrado Alvaro, *Calabria*, Nemi, Firenze; n. ed. con pref. di L. Bigiaretti e un saggio di D. Scafoglio, Qualecultura Jaca Book, Vibo Valentia 1990. Alvaro, C. 1990b, *Un treno nel Sud* (1958), introduzione di V. Teti, n. ed. Rubbettino, Soveria Mannelli, 2017.

Corrado Alvaro, *Gente in Aspromonte*, Garzanti, Milano, 2017.

Corrado Alvaro, *il nostro tempo e la speranza*. Saggi di vita contemporanea, Bompiani, 1952.

Corrado Alvaro, "Ritratto di Melusina", in *L'Amata alla finestra*. Introduzione di Walter Pedula, bibliografia di Massimo Onofri; I grandi tascabili 347, Milano Bompiani, Fifth edition (1994).

Sumudu Atapattu and Carmen G. gonzalez, "The North–South Divide in International Environmental Law: Framing the Issues", in *International Environmental Law and the Global South*, edited by S. Alam, S. Atapattu, C.G. Gonzalez, and J. Razzaque (Cambridge University Press; 2015), 1–20.

S.O. Atteh, "The Political Economy of Environmental Degradation: The Dumping of Toxic Wastes in West Africa", *The African Review: A Journal of African Politics, Development and International Affairs*, 20(1/2), 19–38, 1993.

Dana Bdier, Guido Veronese, Fayez, and F. Mahamid, "Quality of Life and Mental Health Outcomes: The Role of Sociodemographic Factors in the Palestinian Context", *Sci Rep*, 13, 16422, 2023.

Lauren Berlant, "Slow Death (Sovereignty, Obesity, Lateral Agency)", *Critical Inquiry*, 33(4), 754–780.

Fernand Braudel, "History and the Social Sciences: The Longue Durée", translated by Immanuel Wallerstein, *Review*, 32, 171–203.

102 Bibliography

Edmund Burke, *The Making of the Modern Mediterranean: Views from the South* (Berkeley: University of California Press, 2019).

Tina Campt, *Listening to Images* (Durham/London: Duke University Press, 2017).

Albert Camus and Arthur Goldhammer, *Algerian Chronicles* (Cambridge, MA: Harvard University Press, 2013).

Alessia Candito, "Viaggio a Rosarno sette anni dopo la rivolta", in *La Repubblica.it*, 2017.

Anne Carson, *Economy of the Unlost* (Princeton: Princeton University Press, 1999).

Adriana Cavarero, *In Spite of Plato* (Polity Press, 1995).

Domenico Cersosimo e Sabina Licurdi, *Lento Pede. Vivere nell'Italia estrema* (Donizelli, 2023).

Iain Chambers, *A Fluid Archive*, 2019.

Iain Chambers, *Mediterranean Crossings: The Politics of an Interrupted Modernity* (Durham, NC: Duke University Press, 2008).

Iain Chambers, "Thinking with the Diver. The Mediterranean in Historical Perspective", *The British Academy Library*, 2020.

Iain Chambers, "What is 'Black' in the Black Mediterranean?", *Post-colonial Politics Journal*, 2024.

Iain Chambers and Marta Cariello, "The Mediterranean Question: Thinking with the Diver", *Journal of Mediterranean Knowledge-JMK*, *5*(1), 141–149, 2020.

Hélène Cixous, *"Coming to Writing"* and Other Essays. With an introductory essay by Susan Rubin Suleiman. Edited by Deborah Jenson and translated by Sarah Cornell.

Hélène Cixous, *Readings. The Poetics of Blanchot, Joyce, Kafka, Kleist, Lispector, and Tsvetayeva* (University of Minnesota Press, 1991).

CGIL–FILCAM, "Immigrati, una giornata di guerriglie a Rosarno", report.

Jennifer Clapp, "The Toxic Waste Trade with Less Industrialized Countries: Economic Linkages and Political Alliances", *Third World Quarterly 15*(3), 505–518, 1994.

Roberto Dainotto, "Asimmetrie Mediterranee: Etica e mare nostrum", *NAE*, *3*, 3–18, 2003.

John Dickie, *Cosa Nostra: A History of the Sicilian Mafia* (St. Martin's Griffin; First Edition, October 21, 2005).

Mahmood Darwish, *In The Presence of Absence*, translated by Sinan Antoon (Archipelago Books, 2011).

Mahmood Darwish, *Memory for Forgetfulness*, translated by and with an introduction by Ibrahim Muhawi, and with a new foreword by Sinan Antoon (University California Press, 1995).

Alessandra Di Maio, "Il mediterraneo nero: Rotte dei migranti nel millennio globale", in *La Città Cosmopolita*, edited by Giulia de Spuches (Palermo: Palumbo Editore, 2012), 143–163.

Francesco Donnici and Andrea Carnì, "Jolly Rosso, la nave dei veleni e le anomalie irrisolte", in *Corriere della Calabria*, 2021.

Alaa Abd El-Fattah, *You Have Not Yet Been Defeated* (Seven Stories Press, 2021).

Abdulkadir Egal, "Suspected Correlation between Cancer Incidence and Industrial and Nuclear Wastes in Somalia", *The Horn of Africa*, *XXVII*, 202–218, December 2009.

Nadia Abu El-Haj, *Facts on the Ground: Archaeological Practice and Territorial Self-fashioning in Israeli Society* (Chicago, IL: The University of Chicago Press, 2002).

Gerrit Faber, "International Trade and Environmental Policies", *Environmntal Policy in an International Context*, *3*, 2003, 79–103.

Bibliography 103

Franz Fanon, "Concerning Violence", in *The Wretched of the Earth*, 1961.

Mahdi Fleifel, *Xenos* (2013), 13 mins.

Claudio Fogu, *The Fishing Net and the Spider Web: Mediterranean Imaginaries and the Making of Italians* (Basingstoke: Palgrave Macmillan, 2020).

Claudio Fogu, "We Have Made the Mediterranean; Now We Must Make Mediterraneans", in *Critically Mediterranean: Temporalities, Aesthetics, and Deployments of a Sea in Crisis*, edited by yasser elhariry and Edwige Tamalet Talbayev (Cham: Springer, 2018), 181–197.

Sigmund Freud, "Mourning and Melancholia", in *Standard Edition of the Complete Psychological Works of Sigmund Freud, 14*(1914–1916), edited and translated by James Strachey et al. (London: Hogarth Press), 243–258.

Nouri Gana, *Melancholy Acts: Defeat and Cultural Critique in the Arab World* (New York, NY, 2023; online edition, Fordham Scholarship Online, 18 Jan. 2024).

Sabrina Garofalo, *Donne, violenza e 'ndrangheta. Metodi, storie e politiche* (Novalogos, 2023).

Ernest Gellner and John Waterbury, *Patrons and Clients* (London: Duckworth, 1977).

Ilaria Giglioli, "Unmaking the Mediterranean Border. Mediterraneanism, Colonial Mobilities and Postcolonial Migration", in *Tesi di dottorato* (Berkeley, CA: University of California, 2018).

Eduard Glissant, *Caribbean Discourse* (Caraf Books, 1989).

Eduard Glissant, *Poetics of Relation*, translated by Betsy Wing (University Michigan Press, 1997).

David Graeber, "Value as the Importance of Action", in *La balsa de piedra*, n 6, enero-marzo, 2014.

Greenpeace Italy Report, "The Toxic Ships. The Italian Hub, the Mediterranean Area and Africa", June 2010.

Leonardo Goi, "Us against the World: Jonas Carpignano's Calabrian Trilogy", in *MUBI*, 2022.

Giuseppe Grimaldi, "The Black Mediterranean: Liminality and the Reconsfiguration of Afroeuropeanneess", *Open Cultural Studies*, *3*, 414–427.

Mohammed Haddad, "Nakba Day: What Happened in Palestine in 1948?", *Al Jazeera*, 15 May, 2022.

Fouad Hamdan, *Waste Trade in the Mediterranean: Toxic Attack against Lebanon. Case One: Toxics from Italy* (Green Peace Lebanon, 1996).

Yannis Hamilakis, *The Nation and Its Ruins: Antiquity, Archaeology, and National Imagination in Greece* (Oxford University Press, 2009).

Yannis Hamilakis and Rafael Greenberg, "Modernity's Sacred Ruins: Colonialism, Archaeology, and the National Imagination in Greece and Israel", video, 2021.

Shuruq Harb, *The Jump* (2020), one-channel video, 10 mins.

Shuruq Harb, *The White Elephant* (2018), one-channel video, 12 mins.

Gelina Harlaftis, "Maritime History: A New Version of the Old Version and the True History of the Sea", *International Journal of Maritime History*, *32*(2), 2020, 383–402.

Gelina Harlaftis, "The Onassis Global Shipping Business, 1920s–1950s", *Business History Review*, *88* (Summer 2014), 241–271.

Gelina Harlaftis, Τζελίνα Χαρλαύτη, "Το "κατηγορώ" του Αριστοτέλη Ωνάση προς τους εφοπλιστές και την ελληνική κυβέρνηση το 1947, Ιόνιος Λόγος, 2013.

Saidiya Hartman, "The Anarchy of Colored Girls Assembled in a Riotous Manner", *South Atlantic Quarterly*, *117* (July, 2018): 465–490.

104   *Bibliography*

Saidiya Hartman, *Wayward lives, beautiful Experiments: Intimate Histories of Social Upheavals* (Norton & Company, 2019).

Michael Herzfeld, "Honour and Shame: Problems in the Comparative Analysis of Moral Systems", *Man*, *15*(2), 1980, 339–351.

Zoe A. Holman, "Palestine: From Accord to Apartheid", *The New Internationalist*, 2023.

Bell Hooks, *Killing Rage. Ending Racism* (New York, NY: Henry Holt & Company, 1995).

Peregrine Horden and Nicholas Purcell, *The Corrupting Sea: A Study of Mediterranean History* (WILEY Blackwell, 2020).

Muawya Ahmed Hussein, "Costs of Environmental Degradation: An Analysis in the Middle East and North Africa Region", in *Management of Environmental Quality. An International Journal*, *9*, n. 3, anno, 2008, 305–317.

Alessandro Iacuelli, *Le Vie Infinite Dei Rifiuti—Il Sistema Campano* (Raleigh, 2nd edn, Lulu.Com 2007).

Sean M. Ingalla, "The Profit Behind Israel's Apartheid of Palestine", *Philippine Collegian*, 2023.

International Labour Organization, "Forced Labour, Modern Slavery and Trafficking in Persons" report.

Sintia Issa, "Beyond the Garbage Politics of Emergency: The Paradox of Infrastructural Failure in Beirut's Peripheries", *The World Humanities Report*, 2023.

Sintia Issa, "Waste You Cannot Deny: A Slow Trans-aesthetic in The Blue Barrel Grove", *The Routledge Companion to Contemporary Art, Visual Culture, and Climate Change* (Routledge, 2021).

Tarek Kahlaoui, *Creating the Mediterranean: Maps and the Islamic Imagination* (Amsterdam: Brill, 2018).

Rashid Khalidi, *The Hundred Years' War on Palestine: A History of Settler Colonialism and Resistance, 1917–2017* (Metropolitan Books, 2020).

Colin P. Kelley, Shahrzad Mohtadi, Mark A. Cane, and Yochanan Kushnir, "Climate Change in the Fertile Creescent and Implications of the Recent Syrian Drought", *PNAS Journal*, *112*, n. 11, November 2014.

Tom Kington, "Italians Cheer as Police Move African Immigrants Out after Clashes with Locals", *The Guardian* online, 2010.

Nikos Kosmatopoulos, "A People's Sea: Palestine and Popular Thalassopolitics in the Mediterranean Sea", *Millennium 51*(3), 2023, 739–757.

Ilham Khury Makdisi, *The Eastern Mediterranean and the Making of Global Radicalism, 1860–1914* (University of California Press, 2013).

Max Liboiron, "Waste Colonialism", *Discard Studies* (November 1, 2018).

Mario Liverani, "Imperialism", in *Archaeologies of the Middle East. Critical Perspectives*, edited by S. Pollock and R. Bernbeck (Oxford: Blackwell, 2005), 223–243.

Legambiente, "Le Navi dei Veleni", report, 2011.

Michael Leonardi, "Italy's Secret Ships of Poison", in counterpunch.org, 2009.

Cesare Lombroso, *In Calabria* (1892) (Rubettino, 2019).

Laura Lo Presti, "Like a Map Over Troubled Water: (Un)mapping the Mediterranean Sea's Terraqueous Necropolitics", in *e-flux journal*, Issue #109, May 2020.

Audre Lorde, "For Each of You", in *The Collected Poems of Audre Lorde* (W. W. Norton & Company; Reprint edition, February 17, 2000).

Bibliography 105

Audre Lorde, "The Uses of Anger: Women Respond to Racism", *Sister/Outsider: Essays and Speeches* (Freedom, CA: The Crossing Press, 1984).

Luizabcl, "The North-South Divide and Its Long-Lasting Effects on Italian Culture", in nuitalian.org, April 27, 2023.

Nesrine Malik, "What Does It Mean to Erase a People—A Nation, Culture, Identity? In Gaza, We Are Beginning to Find Out", *The Guardian*, 18 December, 2023.

Alberto Maritati, *La Nave dei Veleni. Il caso Cavtat* (Laterza, 2021).

Nur-eldeen Masalha, *The Palestine Nakba: Decolonising History, Narrating the Subaltern, Reclaiming Memory* (Bloomsbury Publishing, 2012).

Francesco Mastroberti, *La Calabria nel Decennio Francese.Storia di guerra, insurrezione e di anarchia* (Università della Calabria, 2018).

Nabil Matar, *Mediterranean Captivity through Arab Eyes* (Brill, 2021).

Predrag Matvejevic, *Mediterranean. A Cultural Landscape* (University of California Press, 1999).

Chris Milton, "Somalia Used as Toxic Dumping Ground", in *The Ecologist*, 2009.

Trin T. Minh-Ha, *Woman, Native, Other. Writing Postcoloniality and Feminism* (Bloomington, IN and Indianapolis, IN: Indiana University Press, 1989).

Harvey Neptune, "Loving through Loss: Reading Saidiya Hartman's History of Black Hurt", in *Anthurium: A Caribbean Studies Journal*, 6, n. 1, June 2008.

Sianne Ngai, *Ugly Feelings* (Harvard University Press, 2005).

Rob Nixon, *Slow Violence and the Environmentalism of the Poor* (Cambridge, MA and London: Harvard University Press, 2013).

Vanessa Ogle, "Archipelago Capitalism: Tax Havens, Offshore Money, and the State, 1950s–1970s", *American Historical Review*, *122*(5), 1431–1458, December 2017.

Vanessa Ogle, "FUNK MONEY': The End of Empire, The Expansion of Tax-Havens, and Decolonization as Economic and Financial Event", in *Past and Present*, no. 249, November 2020.

Vanessa Ogle, "The End of Empire and the Rise of Tax Havens. How Decolonisation Propelled the Growth of Low-tax Jurisdictions, with Lasting Economic Implications for Former Colonies", in *The New Statesman*, December 2020.

Ilan Pappé, "Israel's Incremental Genocide in the Gaza Ghetto", *The Electronic Intifada*, 2014.

Ilan Pappé, "The 1948 Ethnic Cleansing of Palestine", *Journal of Palestine Studies*, *36*(1), 6–20, 2006.

Domenico Perrotta, 7 Gennaio 2010: La Rivolta di Rosarno, Il Mulino, blog, 2020.

Maria Concetta Preta, *Riprendersi la terra. Angelina Mauro e la strage di Melissa.*

Jasbir K. Puar, *The Right to Maim: Debility, Capacity, Disability* (Duke University Press, 2017).

Nicholas Purcell, *The Liquid Continent: A Study of Mediterranean History* (Blackwell Pub., 2010).

Joan Retallack, *The Poethical Wager* (Berkeley, CA/Los Angeles, CA: University California Press, 2003).

Alex Ritman, "Mahdi Fleifel on His Scorsese-Inspired Palestinian Refugee Thriller to a Land Unknown", *Variety*, July 2024.

Carl Rommel and Joseph John Viscomi, "Introduction: Locating the Mediterranean", in *Locating the Mediterranean: Connections and Separations across Space and Time*, edited by Carl Rommel and Joseph J. Viscomi (Helsinki: Helsinki University Press, 2022), 1–29.

106 *Bibliography*

Edward Said, *The Question of Palestine* (New York, NY: Vintage Books, 1992).

Suja Sawafta, Two Shores, One Sea. Longin for Palestine's Mediterranean, February 28, 2024.

Isabel Schäfer, "The Cultural Dimension of the Euro-Mediterranean Partnership: A Critical Review of the First Decade of Intercultural Cooperation", *History and Anthropology*, *18*(3), 333–352, 2007.

Giulia Sfameni Gasparro, "Aspects of the Cult of Demetra in Magna Grecia", in *Mystic Cults in Magnia Grecia*, edited by G. Casadio, P.A. Johnston (University of Texas Press, 2009).

Adania Shibli, *Minor Detail* (Fitzcarraldo Editions, 2020).

Said Shukri, "The Silent Epidemic: The Toll of Mental Health in Occupied Palestine", *Palestinian Medical and Pharmaceutical Journal*, *8*(1), 2023.

Ann Stoler, "The Rot Remains", *Imperial Debris. On Ruins to Ruination* (Duke University Press, 2013).

Tiziana Terranova and Iain Chambers, "Technology, Postcoloniality, and the Mediterranean", *e-flux Journal*, Issue #123, December 2021.

Vito Teti, *I luoghi e i disastri. Le reti della storia, della natura e degli individui*, in *L'Italia dei disastri dati e riflessioni sull'impatto degli eventi naturali 1861–2013*, edited by E. Guidoboni and G. Valensise (Bologna: Bononia University Press), 359–373.

Vito Teti, *Il vampiro e la melanconia* (Donzelli, 2018). "Mediterraneum. Geografie dell'interno", in *Mediterraneo e cultura europea*, edited by G. Cacciatore, M. Signore, et al. (Rubbettino, Soveria Mannelli, 2003), 107–128.

Vito Teti, *Luoghi, culti, memorie dell'acqua*, in Teti V. (a cura di), 2003; *Il senso dei luoghi. Memoria e vita dei paesi abbandonati*, pref. di P. Matvejevic', Roma, Donzelli (n. ed. aggiornata, ivi, 2014).

Vito Teti, *Maledetto Sud* (Einaudi, 2015).

Vito Teti, *Quel che resta. L'Italia dei paesi, tra abbandono e ritorno* (Donzelli, 2017).

Vito Teti, *Terra inquieta* (Italian Edition) (Rubettino, 2018).

Vito Teti, *Tradizione e modernità nell'opera di Corrado Alvaro*, in A.M. Morace (a cura di), *Corrado Alvaro e la letteratura tra le due guerre* (Pellegrini, Cosenza, 2005), 515–540.

Mihail Tremopoulos, *Shipwrecks Containing Toxic and Nuclear Waste in the Mediterranean*.

Judlirh E. Tucker, *The Making of the Modern Mediterranean. Views from the South* (University of California Press, 2019).

United Nations. UN General Assembly (1948). *Convention on the Prevention and Punishment of the Crime of Genocide* (9 December 1948). United Nations, Treaty Series, vol. 78.

Simone Weil, *Gravity and Grace*, translated by Emma Crawford and Mario von der Ruhr (London: Routledge, 2002), 14.

Louise E. Wise, "Social Death and the Loss of a 'World': An Anatomy of Genocidal Harm in Sudan", *The International Journal of Human Rights*, *21*(7), 838–865, 2017.

Rob White, "Toxic Cities. Globalizing the Problem of Waste", *Social Justice*, *35*(3), 113, *War, Crisis & Transition* (2008–2009), 107–119.

Index

Abd El-Fattah, Alaa 48
accountability 74
active freedom 80
Adnan, Etel 8–9, 54–55, 57
African-American struggle 7
aggressiveness 7, 44–45
Aghasi, Maya 56–57, 60n28
Ahmed, Sara 20, 20n5, 33, 38, 40n1, 42, 47, 49n2–3, 49n17
Ain el-Helweh refugee camp 86
al-Hashem, Joseph 73
alienation 80–82, 85
Alpi, Ilaria 74
Alvaro, Corrado 3, 8–9, 20n1, 40n7, 62, 69n1–3
anger 5–7, 42–43, 47; de-pathologising 7; manifestations 43–44; words for, in Homeric work 44; *see also* feminist, anger
anti-mafia commission 48
archival traces 77
arms trafficking 73
As-Safi 71
asylum seekers 86; *see also* alienation
Atlantique (2019) 86
Atshan, Laila 83

Barnwell, Garret 72
Beirut waterfront 72
Belghazi, Taieb 51
bioproteins 70n14
Blue Barrel Grove, The (2014-ongoing) 73
"blue barrels" 73–74
border violence 81
Braudel, Fernand 59n8
Bueti, Angela, disappearance 2–4, 27–31, 33
Busan Biennale Committee 98n2

Calabria Napoleonica 45
Calabrians 65
Campania 71–72
Camus, Albert 51, 59n2
cancer 72
capitalist destruction 72–73
Capo Spartivento 71
carcinogenic manufacturing 77
Caribbean Discourse 91
Cariello, Marta 54
Carpignano, Jonas 68
Cavarero, Adriana 44, 49n7
Celan, Paul 34
Chambers, Iain 5, 53–54, 60n10–12, 60n15–17
Cirillo, Mary 29
Ci sono storie di donne (Primerano) 58
civil war: in Lebanon 73; in Syria 72
Cixous, Hélène 7, 34, 40n5–6
Clement of Alexandria 44
coercion 21
collective punishment 83
Colonial archaeology 66
colonial history 90
colonialism 96
colonial melancholization 37
colonisation 4–5
Coming to Writing (Cixous) 34
contaminations 90
control 21
Corrado, Alvaro 34
creativity 85–86
creolisation 6
criminal: acts 31; mentality 28; violence 75–76
criminalisation 81
criminality 2
crisis 82

108 *Index*

crossing 90
cultural heritage 82
cultural identity 64
cultural manifestations 56
cultural or educational initiatives, absence of 81
cultural supremacy 52

Dainotto, Roberto 51, 59n4
Darwish, Mahmoud 12n1, 80
Darwish, Wafa 83
"death deal" 71–78
debilitation 83
debility 82–83
decolonial melancholicization 37
decolonisation 52, 60n9, 91, 95–96
De Grazia, Natale 74
dehumanisation 47
dehumanising practices of nation-states 82
Demeter (Greek goddess) 43–44
de-pathologising anger 7
depression 5, 82–83
Depth Unknown 66
Díaz-Andreu, Margarita 67
Dickie, John 46, 49n16
Dino, Alessandra 30
Diop, Mati 86
disappearance, act of 84
displacement 72
dispossession 82, 98
domination, system of 1
double violence 28
dreaming 80

economic and social collapse 81
economic crisis 53
emotional and cognitive abilities 82
emotional dispositions 6
environmental crimes 76
environmental degradation 72
environmental violence 73
epistemic violence 3
exemplary punishment 30
Eyad, Abu 6, 9, 86–87

family capital 94
Fanon, Franz 4–7, 36, 52–53, 59n1, 59n5–6
fascism 4
feeling of being stuck 90
feminicide 30; *see also* violence against women
feminism 33, 42
feminist: anger 42; sadness 38

financial crisis 77
Fishing Net, The (Fogu) 64
Fleifel, Fleifel 9
Fleifel, Mahdi 9, 81, 86–87
floating museum 93, 98
Fogu, Claudio 4, 64, 67
Fortunati, Giustino 62–63
freedom 86
free-market capitalism 96
French colonization 64
French protectorate in Tunisia 64
Freud, Sigmund 33–34, 40n4
Frisina, Augusta 29, 31n3

Gana, Nouri 7, 36–38, 41n11–17
garbage crisis 77
Garofalo, Lea 30
Garofalo, Sabrina 28, 31n1, 32n6–8
Garrone, Matteo 86
Gasparro, Giulia Sfameni 49n6
Gaza 37, 82
geography of toxicities 71
Giglioli, Ilaria 64, 69n4
Glissant, Edouard 1, 6, 12n2, 90–91, 99n5
global economic interests 95
Goi, Leonardo 70n15
Goldhammer, Arthur 59n2
Graeber, David 80
Greece 1
Greece's economic crisis 87
Greek maritime power 92
Greek ship-owners 97
Greek shipping aristocracy 94

Hades (Greek god) 43
Hamilakis, Yannis 65, 67, 69n5
Harb, Shuruq 9, 11, 80–81, 83, 98n2
Harlaftis, Gelina 11, 92
Harrison, Olivia 59, 61n31
Hartman, Saidiya 6, 77
Heleta, Savo 72
Hellas Liberty Museum 93
Hillesum, Hetty 34
Hirsch, Marianne 38
Historic Palestine 91
Hrovatin, Miran 74
humanity 83
Human Rights Watch 77
humiliation 21; of checkpoints 82
hybridisation 6

I Couldn't but Dance (2014) 73
illegal landfills 71

Index 109

imagining 81
immigration 53
immobility 80–81
immobilization 81–82
In Calabria (Lombroso) 45
incapacitation 83
inconsistencies 73
industrialisation 63
infidelity 29
infrastructural failures 72
intergenerational links 82
International Labour Organization 49n21
intimidation 2
intolerable human misery 12
Io Capitano (2023) 86
Issa, Sintia 72, 76–77
Italian mafia groups 73
Italian unification 64

"Jolly Rosso" 74
Jump, The (2018) 10
Jump, The (2021) 83
jumping 84

Kanafani, Ghassan 37–38
Khatibi, Abdelkebir 51
Khazrik, Jessika 9, 73–74, 76–78
kidnappings 43, 55
"King of Waste" 71
Kington, Tom 49n20

La Corsa dell'Innocente (1992) 67
language and imagination 80
Lanzino, Roberta 29
Lear, Jonathan 84
Lebanese Christian masculinity 55
Lebanese civil war 59
Lebanon 1, 77
liberation, struggle of 7
Liberty 93–95, 97
Liberty Hellas Museum 11
Liberty ship 11
Liquichimica Biosintesi 67
liquid continent 81–82
liquid imaginaries of journeying 90
liquidity of the sea 90
Lispector, Clarice 34
Lombroso, Cesare 45
Lo Presti, Laura 81–82
Lorde, Audre 7, 42, 49n1, 49n4

Maledetto Sud (Teti) 4, 45
marginalisation 83

marginality and alienation 85
marital contract 29
mass-migration 63
Matvejevic, Predrag 5
Mediterranean 8, 48; community 4–6,
    51–52; culture 52
Mediterranean Question, The (Chamber
    and Cariello) 54
Mediterranean Sea 83–84
megara 44
melancholia 82–83
melancholy 7; disposition 5; militant
    inhabitation of 36; subjectivity 36
Melancholy Acts (Gana) 7, 36
Memmi, Albert 51
mental health: challenges 72; disorders
    and disabilities 82–83
Middle-Eastern refugees 86
migrants 86; *see also* alienation
Minor Detail (Shibli) 8, 38–39
modernisation 35
Mount Mound Refuse (2016–2022) 9,
    73–75
mourn, refusal to 33
Mourning and Melancholia (Freud)
    33–34
murder 57
Mysteries 44

nationalism 95
nationalist discourse 91
national taxation 95–96
*Nation and Its Ruins: Antiquity,
    Archaeology, and National
    Imagination in Greece, The*
    (Hamilakis) 65
natural catastrophes 62
'ndrangheta 2, 28, 30–31, 46, 68
ndranghetista 50n15
neo-colonialism 96
neutrality of language 76
Nixon, Bob 71
Nixon, Rob 40n2, 78n5
Nizhny Novgorod 70n15
nomadism 90
normalised violence 2
Norman-Swabian castle of Squillace 65
North-eastern Syria 72

obsession 28
offshore and decolonisation 96–97
"Off You Paper Trail" (2024) 97n1, 98n2
Off You Shore Paper Trail, 2024 90

110   *Index*

Ogle, Vanessa 11, 95
Omar, Abdaljawad 80
Onassis 93
oppression 1, 5
Orientalism (Said) 52
Oslo Accord 84

Palestine 1, 8, 82
Palestine-Israel conflict 55
Palestinian liberation 38
Palestinian refugees 9–10; camps 55
Parthenon marbles 66
patriarchal culture 28
patterns of colonialism 53
Paur, Jasbir 82–83
Penal Code, art. 587 31n4
perennial crisis 5
performance of violence 57
Perrella, Nunzio 71
Perrotta, Domenico 49n18–19
Pesce, Giuseppina 30
physical and mental exhaustion 81
physical and psychological
    malformations 72
physical destruction 72
poison ships 72
politics of immobility 81–82
Portrait of Melusina (Corrado) 34
post-war Europe 91, 95
powerlessness 8
Preta, Maria Concetta 46, 49n13, 50n14
Primerano, Nando 58, 61n32
punishment 83; of movement 81

racism 7, 33
radical feminists 7
radioactive waste 73
rape 29, 43; *see also* violence against
    women
refugees 53; crisis 87
refusal to recognize a system 5, 42
Reggio Calabria 1, 27, 64, 67–68,
    70n13, 90
Reggio riots 68
reparatory marriage 29
resignation 82–83
*Right to Maim: Debility, Capacity,
    Disability, The* (2017) 82–83
Right to Maim, The (Puar) 10
*Riprendersi la terra. Angelina Mauro e
    la strage di Melissa* (Preta) 46
Romeo, Angelina 46

Rommel, Carl 59n3
Rose, Marie 6, 54–55, 57–58
Rothberg, Michael 12n5
ruination 67
ruins 62–69

sadness 36, 40
sadness, intensification of 33
Said, Edward 52
Sawafta, Suja 92
Schäfer, Isabelle 53
Sciarra I 15–20
Sciarra II 27–31
sense of abandonment 81
sense of alienation 36
sense of freedom 83
sense of stuckness 90
sexism 33
shared feeling 90
shared home 90
Shibli, Adania 8–9, 38–39, 41n19
shipwrecks 94–95
Sicilians 65
silent epidemic 82
sinking ships 71
Sitt Marie Rose (Adnan) 9, 54
slow death 82
"slow violence" 71
social collapse 86
Somalia 72
staged execution 56
state violence 77
Stoler, Ann 67
structural inequities 31
structural violence 7, 31, 81; *see also*
    violence
suicide 82–84

tax-free locations 96
tax heaven 95–97
Terranova, Tiziana 53, 60n10–12
territorial dismemberment 84–85
Teti, Vito 2–3, 20n4, 30–31, 45, 63
Thesmophoria 44
toxic substances, illegal dumping of 71–72
transcolonial Mediterranean 59
transformation 90
traumas in conflict zones 72

Ulysses 19
United Nations Population Fund 82
urbanisation 63

Index 111

violence 2, 7, 30, 43, 55–56, 71–72, 81–82; history of 7; normalising 38; structural 7
violence against women 28–29; normalisation of 2; private 30; public 30
Viscomi, Joseph 51, 59n3

water scarcity 72
Weil, Simone 33, 38, 40n3, 41n18
West Bank 83, 92

Western civilisation 53
White Elephant, The (2018) 10, 84
witnessing violence 3
Wretched of the Eartk (Fanon) 4

Xavier, Giovanni 45
Xenos (2014) 9, 86

Zeus (Greek god) 43
Zionism 66

9781032795423